HAPPINESS
around the World

HAPPINESS
around the world

the paradox of happy peasants
and miserable millionaires

CAROL GRAHAM

OXFORD
UNIVERSITY PRESS

OXFORD
UNIVERSITY PRESS

Great Clarendon Street, Oxford OX2 6DP

Oxford University Press is a department of the University of Oxford.
It furthers the University's objective of excellence in research, scholarship,
and education by publishing worldwide in

Oxford New York

Auckland Cape Town Dar es Salaam Hong Kong Karachi
Kuala Lumpur Madrid Melbourne Mexico City Nairobi
New Delhi Shanghai Taipei Toronto

With offices in

Argentina Austria Brazil Chile Czech Republic France Greece
Guatemala Hungary Italy Japan Poland Portugal Singapore
South Korea Switzerland Thailand Turkey Ukraine Vietnam

Oxford is a registered trade mark of Oxford University Press
in the UK and in certain other countries

Published in the United States
by Oxford University Press Inc., New York

British Library Cataloguing in Publication Data

Data available

Library of Congress Cataloging-in-Publication Data

Graham, Carol, 1962–
Happiness around the world : the paradox of happy peasants and
miserable millionaires / Carol Graham.
p. cm.
ISBN 978-0-19-954905-4 (hbk.)
1. Economics—Psychological aspects. 2. Happiness—Economic aspects.
3. Quality of life. 4. Well-being. I. Title.
HB74.P8G73 2009
305.5—dc22   2009041062

Typeset by SPI Publisher Services, Pondicherry, India
Printed in Great Britain
on acid-free paper by
Clays Ltd., St Ives Plc

ISBN 978-0-19-954905-4

1 3 5 7 9 10 8 6 4 2

In memory of my father,
who mastered the art of finding happiness
in trying to make the world a better place

PREFACE

I could not have written this book without the support and feedback of any number of wonderful colleagues, both at Brookings and beyond. Many of them provided detailed comments on specific chapters or sections of the book over the past year or two. These include: Henry Aaron, George Akerlof, Jere Behrman, Nancy Birdsall, François Bourguignon, Gary Burtless, Mauricio Cardenas, Andrew Clark, Nicholas Cristakis, Angus Deaton, Shanta Devarajan, Ed Diener, Paul Dolan, Steven Durlauf, Richard Easterlin, Joshua Epstein, Andrew Felton, Chico Ferreira, Cliff Gaddy, Ross Hammond, Matthew Hoover, Daniel Kahneman, Charles Kenny, Jeffrey Kling, Robert Litan, Eduardo Lora, Branko Milanovic, Philip Musgrove, Moises Naim, Andrew Oswald, George Perry, Tom Schelling, Alois Stutzer, Ted Truman, and Peyton Young. There are also sections of the book that draw on papers or articles co-authored with a number of very able research assistants or Ph.D. students, who have since gone on to bigger and better things. I benefited greatly from working with them in the interim. They are: Soumya Chattopadhyay, Andrew Eggers, Andrew Felton, Matthew Hoover, Stefano Pettinato, Mario Picon, and Sandip Sukhtankar.

There are also a number of people, both at Brookings and beyond, who provided important intellectual or moral support throughout the process.

PREFACE

Strobe Talbott gave the research a boost of intellectual and moral support when he walked into my office on one of his first visits to Brookings in 2002, curious to know why I was studying happiness. He has supported the research ever since. John Steinbruner has for years provided intellectual inspiration for this, as well as much of my earlier, research. Carlos Pascual gave the research an enormous vote of confidence when he encouraged me to return full time to Brookings in 2008, and allowed me to sit in the Robinson Chair. Chuck Robinson himself has been a supporter since then. Richard Easterlin has been an appreciative reader of virtually anything that I produce, and his feedback and kind invitations to participate in any number of wonderful conferences on happiness economics have been invaluable. Alan Angell of Oxford has never failed to read a paper or chapter without wonderfully healthy skepticism and constant corrections of grammatical error (or 'Americanisms'), which surely improved the end product. Nancy Truitt of the Tinker Foundation has always taken a particular interest in the research, and also managed to engineer essential financial support for the project at critical junctures. Marta Lagos of the Latinobarometro has been exceptionally generous in allowing me constant access to the data set. Jim Clifton of the Gallup Organization and his entire team—including Jim Harter, Gale Muller, and Jesus Rios—have also been generous both via interest in the work and in providing access to the Gallup World Poll data.

At Brookings, a number of people have provided invaluable administrative and other forms of support, an often thankless task, which is at the same time critical to getting anything done. They include Charlotte Baldwin, Yami Fuentes, Linda Gianessi, Sara Hommel, Sun Kordel, and Maggie Kozak. At Oxford University Press, both Sarah Caro and Aimee Wright have been wonderfully patient and brilliantly helpful.

PREFACE

Finally, I cannot close without thanking a number of family members and friends without whom I could not have gotten this done. They provided me with invaluable moral support and friendship, whether by driving carpool at the last minute or just listening to my excitement about having finally gotten data from Afghanistan and/or getting my crime regressions to work. They include Charlotte Baldwin, Elizabeth Davis, Anita Graham and John Schenkel, Berta Gilbert, Alec and Laurie Graham, Bill Hall, Merrill Hall, Pam Hoehn-Saric, Rosa Miranda, Marianne Moxon, and Carol Wise. And, of course, I have to thank my three wonderful children, Alexander, Anna, and Adrian, who are the roots of my happiness. I thank them for being the wonderful individuals that they are and for having the capacity to answer for me when they asked a question and I was plugged into the computer: 'I know, I know, you are trying to finish your book'.

CONTENTS

CONTENTS

CONTENTS

LIST OF FIGURES

LIST OF TABLES

LIST OF TABLES

ABBREVIATIONS

ACSO	Afghanistan's Central Statistics Office
CESD	Center for Epidemiological Studies depression scale
CPI	consumer price index
ECLAC	United Nations Economic Commission for Latin America and the Caribbean
ELQ	economic ladder question
EQ-5D	Euro-Quality-5 Dimensions
FSU	former Soviet Union
GDP	gross domestic product
GNP	gross national product
GSS	General Social Survey
IADB	Inter-American Development Bank
IDASA	Institute for Democracy in South Africa
LDC	less developed country
OLS	ordinary least squares
PCA	principal components analysis
POUM	prospects of upward mobility

ABBREVIATIONS

PPP	purchasing power parity
QALY	quality-adjusted life year
RLMS	Russian Longitudinal Monitoring Survey
SES	socio-economic status
TTO	time trade-offs
UNDP	United Nations Development Programme
USAID	US Agency for International Development

Introduction

So Midas, king of Lydia, swelled at first with pride when he found he could transform everything he touched to gold; but when he beheld his food grow rigid and his drink harden into golden ice then he understood that this gift was a bane and in his loathing for gold, cursed his prayer.

Claudian, In Rufinem

What makes people happy? This is an age-old question, which over time has captured the attention of philosophers, historians, psychologists, and, most recently, economists. King Midas sought happiness in gold, and, in the end, that pursuit made him miserable. How often do we hear the phrase: 'more money does not make you happy'? Yet if money does not make people happy, what does? Does money matter at all? Where and how does the average person find happiness? Given the diversity of people, countries, and cultures across the world, can we even venture an answer to that question?

For decades and indeed centuries, the pursuit of happiness was limited to constitutional proclamations and its study to the ephemeral texts of philosophers. More recently, though, there has been a burgeoning interest in research on happiness. This interest is evident in the social sciences—particularly economics and psychology—and in the media. Perhaps it was a reaction to the decade of the 'me' generation and of the emergence of billionaire CEOs. In retrospect, it may provide a good framework through which to analyze the ensuing economic collapse. Or it may be simply a reflection of how much more adventurous and eclectic the so-called 'dismal science' has become. While no serious economist would have used the word happiness in a scholarly paper three decades ago, the number of publications with happiness in the title in economics journals had well passed the one thousand mark by 2007.[1] Study after study on happiness is cited in news reports across countries, whether about what makes particular cohorts, like teens or women, happy or about which countries are happy and which are sad. The study of happiness is increasingly recognized as a science, and there is serious discussion of applying its findings to policy questions, and even of the development of national well-being indicators to complement GNP data.

Why all the interest? Can we really answer the question what makes people happy? Can it really be proved with credible methods and data? Is there consistency in the determinants of happiness across cohorts, countries, and cultures? Are happiness levels innate to individuals or can policy and the environment people live in make a difference? How is happiness affected by poverty or progress? Is happiness a viable objective for policy? If so, how do we define happiness in a way that is meaningful to policy but still is general enough to compare across cohorts, cultures, and countries?

[1] For one review of this progress, see Clark et al. (2008).

INTRODUCTION

I attempt to answer these questions in this book, based on my own research with several colleagues, as well as on the work of other scholars working in the field. The research takes advantage of the analytical and research tools that are provided by new approaches in economics, as well as from extensive work on the topic by psychologists. These tools allow researchers to address questions that are not well answered by standard revealed preference-based (e.g. consumption choices) approaches in economics, such as the welfare effects of macro and institutional arrangements that individuals are powerless to change, and the explanation of behaviors that are not driven by choice but rather by norms, addiction, or self-control problems.

In the first chapter, I review the theory and concepts of happiness, and how they have evolved historically. I explain how they underpin a new line of research which is, on the one hand, an attempt to understand the determinants of happiness and, on the other, the development of a tool—based on happiness surveys—for understanding the effects of a host of phenomena on human well-being. I also discuss the methods used by economists who study happiness. The second chapter addresses one of the most fundamental questions in happiness research and one over which there is still much debate: the relationship between happiness and income. It highlights how different conclusions can be drawn depending on the methods and data used to study it and identifies some of the methodological challenges involved in the study of happiness.

The third chapter of the book reviews the correlates of happiness in large population samples around the world. These are surprisingly consistent across countries, regardless of their economic development level. I report the results of my research on happiness—as well as that of some others—in countries as diverse as Chile and Kazakhstan, Peru and

Russia, and the United States and Afghanistan. The chapter also identifies some traits which seem specific to particular cohorts and countries or regions.

Chapter 4 asks the question 'does happiness matter?' In other words, does happiness matter to outcomes that we care about, such as in the labor market or health arenas? It explores the effects of happiness on future incomes, on health, and on the probabilities of being married, employed, and of quitting or starting smoking, based on an over time data set for Russia. My co-authors—Andrew Eggers and Sandip Sukhtankar—and I find that happiness does matter to some outcomes that we care about, such as higher levels of income and better health, but not to others.

The fifth chapter is devoted to health, one of the most important variables in the human well-being or happiness equation. It reviews what we know about the relationship between happiness and health, and how it varies according to income levels, health status, and societal norms across countries. It also provides an example of how happiness surveys can contribute to novel measures of well-being, in this case providing a new method for valuing different health states based on life and health satisfaction equations.

The sixth chapter presents what we know about the effects of macroeconomic trends and patterns—ranging from economic growth and financial market crises to inequality, inflation, and unemployment—on happiness. The seventh explores the role of different institutional arrangements, such as political regimes and social networks, as well as that of phenomena, such as crime and corruption. It places particular focus on how individuals adapt to both good and bad equilibriums, via changes in norms and expectations, and discusses the implications of adaptation for both individual and collective welfare.

INTRODUCTION

The final chapter of the book discusses the potential of happiness surveys to contribute to better public policy. The approach provides a broader picture of the determinants of human welfare than that provided by income-based measures, thereby complementing those measures. It also allows scholars to attach relative weights to the various determinants of well-being, such as how much individuals value health or a stable marriage as compared to income. Such information can surely inform policy choices. Yet the chapter also sounds a note of caution, raising a number of conceptual and empirical challenges that must still be addressed prior to considering a more direct application of the findings of happiness studies to policy. Unresolved issues include the appropriate definition of happiness, how to deal with variance in innate happiness levels and in human capacity to adapt to both prosperity and adversity, inter-temporal problems, and a range of normative questions about which happiness levels should be the priority of policy—for example, misery versus less than complete happiness, and/or the unhappiness of the rich versus marginal increases in the happiness of the poor.

CHAPTER 1

The Economics of Happiness[1]

In this first chapter, I briefly review the theory and concepts of happiness and how they have evolved historically. These concepts underpin a new line of research which is, on the one hand, an attempt to understand the determinants of happiness and, on the other, the development of a tool—based on happiness surveys—for understanding the effects of a host of phenomena on human well-being. I briefly review the methods used by economists who study happiness and are using happiness surveys as a research tool. A basic understanding of these methods will be helpful to readers in interpreting the results of the surveys from around the world that I discuss throughout the book.

The economics of happiness is an approach to assessing welfare which combines the techniques typically used by economists with those more commonly used by psychologists. While psychologists have long used surveys of reported well-being to study happiness, economists only recently

[1] This chapter draws heavily on my chapter in Durlauf and Blume, eds. (2008) in the *New Palgrave Dictionary of Economics*, 2nd edn.

ventured into this arena. Early economists and philosophers, ranging from Aristotle to Bentham, Mill, and Smith, incorporated the pursuit of happiness in their work. Yet, as economics grew more rigorous and quantitative, more parsimonious definitions of welfare took hold. Utility was taken to depend only on income as mediated by individual choices or preferences within a rational individual's monetary budget constraint.

Even within a more orthodox framework, focusing purely on income can miss key elements of welfare. People have different preferences for material and non-material goods. They may choose a lower-paying but more personally rewarding job, for example. They are nonetheless acting to 'maximize utility' in the neoclassical economics sense.

The study of happiness or subjective well-being is part of a more general move in economics that challenges these narrow assumptions. The introduction of bounded rationality—which posits that most people are only as rational as their available information, environment, and intellect permit—and the establishment of behavioral economics have opened new lines of research. Happiness economics—which represents one new direction—relies on more expansive notions of utility and welfare, including interdependent utility functions, procedural utility, and the interaction between rational and non-rational influences in determining economic behavior.

Richard Easterlin was the first modern economist to revisit the concept of happiness, beginning in the early 1970s. More generalized interest took hold in the late 1990s, and a number of economists began to study happiness and its relationship with a number of variables of interest, ranging from income, socio-demographic variables, and employment status to the nature of political regimes, the level of economic development, and the scope and quality of public goods, among others

7

(see Blanchflower and Oswald, 2004; Clark and Oswald, 1994; Easterlin, 1974, 2003; Frey and Stutzer, 2002a; Graham and Pettinato, 2002a; Layard, 2005).

The Approach

The economics of happiness does not purport to replace income-based measures of welfare but instead to complement them with broader measures of well-being. These measures are based on the results of large-scale surveys, across countries and over time, of hundreds of thousands of individuals who are asked to assess their own welfare. The surveys provide information about the importance of a range of factors which affect well-being, including income but also others, such as health, marital and employment status, and civic trust.

The approach, which relies on expressed preferences rather than on revealed choices, is particularly well suited to answering questions in areas where a revealed preferences approach provides limited information. Indeed, it often uncovers discrepancies between expressed and revealed preferences. Standard economics relies on revealed preferences—typically measured by consumption choices—as a gauge of individual welfare. Indeed, for many years, economists shied away from survey data—for example, expressed preferences. The assumption was that these data could not be trusted: there is no consequence to answering surveys, as opposed to the trade-offs involved in making consumption choices. Yet revealed preferences cannot fully gauge the welfare effects of particular policies or institutional arrangements which individuals are powerless to change. Examples of these include the welfare effects of inequality, environmental degradation, and macroeconomic policies, such as inflation and unemployment. Sen's capabilities-based approach to poverty, for example, highlights the lack of capacity of the poor to make choices or to take certain actions. In many of his writings, Sen (1995) criticizes economists' excessive focus on choice as a sole indicator of human behavior. Another area where a choice approach is limited and happiness surveys can shed light is the welfare effects of addictive behaviors, such as smoking and drug abuse.

Happiness surveys are based on questions in which the individual is asked, 'Generally speaking, how happy are you with your life?' or 'how satisfied are you with your life?', with possible answers on a four to seven-point scale. Psychologists have a preference for life satisfaction questions. Yet answers to happiness and life satisfaction questions correlate quite closely. The correlation coefficient between the two—based on research on British data for 1975–1992, which includes both questions, and Latin American data for 2000–2001, in which alternative phrasing was used in different years—ranges between 0.56 and 0.50 (Blanchflower and Oswald, 2004; Graham and Pettinato, 2002a).

Differences in the phrasing of happiness questions present several methodological challenges. The particular kind of happiness question that is used matters to the results. For example, respondents' income level seems to matter more to their answers to life satisfaction questions than it does to their answers to questions which are designed to gauge the innate character component of happiness (affect), as gauged by questions such as 'how many times did you smile yesterday?' (for a fuller description of these issues, see Chapter 2 of this book). In more technical terms, the correlation between life satisfaction questions and income is much stronger than that between affect questions and income.

Happiness questions are also particularly vulnerable to order bias—in other words, where they are placed in a survey. People will respond differently to an open-ended happiness question that is at the beginning of a survey than to one that is framed or biased by the questions posed beforehand, such as those about whether income is sufficient or the quality of their job. To minimize this, happiness or life satisfaction questions must be placed at the beginning of surveys. And, as with all economic measurements, any individual's answer may be biased by idiosyncratic, unobserved events (ranging from the break-up of a relationship to the victory of a favorite team in football on the day that the respondent answers a survey).

Bias in answers to happiness surveys can also result from unobserved personality traits and related errors which affect how the same individuals answer a range of questions. A naturally curmudgeonly person, for example, will answer all sorts of questions in a manner that is more negative than the average. (These concerns can be addressed via econometric techniques if and when we have data that observe the same respondents more than one time.) Related concerns about unobservable variables are common to all economic disciplines, and not unique to the study of happiness. For example, a naturally cheerful person may respond to policy measures differently and/or put more effort in the labor market than the average. Standard analysis would attribute those outcomes to differences in incentives rather than in character, which would introduce error into the resulting conclusions.

Despite the potential pitfalls, cross-sections of large samples across countries and over time find remarkably consistent patterns in the determinants of happiness. Psychologists, meanwhile, find validation in the way that people answer these surveys based in physiological measures of happiness, such as the frontal movements in the brain and in the number of 'genuine'—Duchenne—smiles (Diener and Seligman, 2004).

The data in happiness surveys are analyzed via standard econometric techniques, with an error term that captures the unobserved characteristics and error described above.[2] Because the answers to happiness surveys are ordinal rather than cardinal, they are best analyzed via ordered logistic or probability (probit) equations. These equations depart from standard regression equations, which explore a continuous relationship between variables (e.g., happiness and income), and instead explore the probability that an individual will place him or herself in a particular category, typically ranging from unhappy to very happy. These regressions typically yield a lower R-squared—for example, explanatory power—than economists are used to. This reflects the extent to which emotions and other components of true well-being are driving the results, as opposed to the variables that we are able to measure, such as income, education, and marital and employment status.

The availability of panel data—for example, surveys that repeatedly interview the same people over time—in some instances, as well as advances in econometric techniques, are increasingly allowing for sounder analysis (Van Praag and Ferrer-i-Carbonell, 2004).[3] While it is impossible to measure the precise effects of independent variables on true well-being, happiness researchers have used the coefficients on these variables as a

[2] Microeconometric happiness equations have the standard form: $W_{it} = \alpha + \beta x_{it} + \varepsilon_{it}$, where W is the reported well-being of individual i at time t, and x is a vector of known variables, including socio-demographic and socio-economic characteristics. Unobserved characteristics and measurement errors are captured in the error term.

[3] The coefficients produced from ordered probit or logistic regressions are remarkably similar to those from OLS regressions based on the same equations, allowing us to substitute OLS equations for ordered logit or probit and then attach relative weights to them. For an extensive and excellent discussion of the methodology underpinning happiness studies—and how it is evolving—see Van Praag and Ferrer-i-Carbonell (2004).

basis for assigning relative weights to them. They can estimate how much income a typical individual in the United States or United Kingdom would need to produce the same change in stated happiness that comes from the well-being loss resulting from, for example, divorce ($100,000) or job loss ($60,000) (Blanchflower and Oswald, 2004).

The Easterlin Paradox

In his original study, Easterlin (1974) revealed a paradox that sparked interest in the topic but is as yet unresolved. While most happiness studies find that *within* countries wealthier people are, on average, happier than poor ones, studies across countries and over time find very little, if any, relationship between increases in per capita income and average happiness levels. On average, wealthier countries (as a group) are happier than poor ones (as a group); happiness seems to rise with income up to a point, but not beyond it. Yet even among the less happy, poorer countries, there is not a clear relationship between average income and average happiness levels, suggesting that many other factors—including cultural traits—are at play (see Figure 1.1).

More recently, there has been renewed debate over whether there is an Easterlin paradox or not. A number of scholars, such as Angus Deaton, and Betsey Stevenson and Justin Wolfers, have published papers demonstrating a clear relationship between per capita incomes and average happiness levels, with no sign that the correlation weakens, either as income levels increase or over time.[4] Indeed, the work of both sets of authors suggests that the slope may be steeper for richer countries, most likely because

---

[4] This is with a log-linear specification. Deaton (2008); Stevenson and Wolfers (2008).

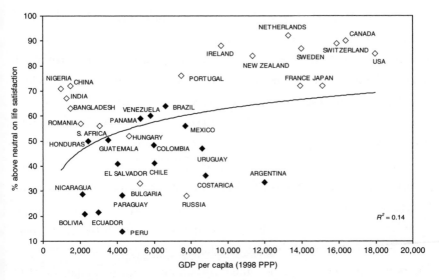

Figure 1.1 Happiness and income per capita, 1990s

Source: Carol Graham and Stefano Pettinato (2002). *Happiness and Hardship: Opportunity and Insecurity in New Market Economies*. Washington, D.C.: The Brookings Institution.

wealthier people are better able to enjoy higher levels of income than are poor ones (a greed effect?).[5] Both of these studies rely on the newly available Gallup World Poll, which covers over 120 countries worldwide, as well as some different data sets for earlier years. Ron Inglehart, meanwhile, in a new analysis of data from the World Values Survey for 1981–2006 finds that subjective well-being rose in 77% of the 52 countries for which time series data are available.[6] Eduardo Lora and colleagues at the Inter-American Development Bank, using Gallup data for Latin America,

[5] Deaton gets a positive and significant coefficient on a squared specification of the income variable. Stevenson and Wolfers split their sample into those countries above and below $15,000 per capita (in year 2000 US dollars); they get a slightly steeper slope for the rich countries than for the poor ones.

[6] Inglehart et al. (2008).

also find a positive relationship between per capita income levels and average happiness levels.[7]

Other studies come out somewhere in the middle. My own work with Stefano Pettinato—the first study of happiness in a large sample of developing countries, using absolute levels of per capita GDP, finds that, on average, happiness levels are higher in the developed than in the developing countries in the sample, but that *within* each group of countries, there is no clear income–happiness relationship (see Figure 1.1). Our work is based on the World Values Survey and on the Latinobarometro poll for Latin America.

Why the discrepancy? For a number of reasons—many of them methodological—the divergent conclusions may each be correct. The relationship between happiness and income is mediated by a range of factors that can alter its slope and/or functional form. These include the particular questions that are used to measure happiness; the selection of countries that is included in the survey sample; the specification of the income variable (log or linear); the rate of change in economic conditions in addition to absolute levels; and changing aspirations as countries go from the ranks of developing to developed economies. The relationship between income and happiness—as well as the various factors mediating it—are discussed in detail in Chapter 3.

There is much less debate about the relationship between income and happiness within countries. Income matters to happiness (Diener et al., 1993; Oswald, 1997, among others). Deprivation and abject poverty in particular are very bad for happiness. Yet after basic needs are met, other factors, such as rising aspirations, relative income differences, and the security of gains,

---

[7] Inter-American Development Bank (2008).

become increasingly important, in addition to income. Long before the economics of happiness was established, James Duesenberry (1949) noted the impact of changing aspirations on income satisfaction and its potential effects on consumption and savings rates. A number of happiness studies have since confirmed the effects of rising aspirations, and have also noted their potential role in driving excessive consumption and other perverse economic behaviors (Frank, 1999).

Thus, a common interpretation of the Easterlin paradox is that humans are on a 'hedonic treadmill': aspirations increase along with income and, after basic needs are met, relative rather than absolute levels of income matter to well-being. Another interpretation of the paradox is the psychologists' 'set point' theory of happiness, in which every individual is presumed to have a happiness level that he or she goes back to over time, even after major events such as winning the lottery or getting divorced (Easterlin, 2003). The implication of this theory for policy is that nothing much can be done to increase happiness.

Individuals are remarkably adaptable, no doubt, and in the end can get used to most things, and in particular to income gains. Adaptation—to both good and bad equilibriums—and how it varies across development levels is a theme which runs throughout the various chapters of this book. The behavioral economics literature, meanwhile, shows that individuals value losses more than gains (see Kahneman et al., 1999, among others). Easterlin argues that individuals adapt more in the income or financial arenas than in non-income-related arenas, while life-changing events, such as bereavement, have lasting effects on happiness. Yet, because most policy is based on pecuniary measures of well-being, it overemphasizes the importance of income gains to well-being and underestimates that of other factors, such as health, family, and stable employment.

There is no consensus about which interpretation is most accurate. Yet numerous studies which demonstrate that happiness levels can change significantly in response to a variety of factors suggest that the research can yield insights into human well-being which provide important, if complementary, information for policymakers. Even under the rubric of set point theory, happiness levels can fall significantly in the aftermath of events like illness or unemployment. Even if levels eventually adapt upwards to a longer-term equilibrium, mitigating or preventing the unhappiness and disruption that individuals experience for months, or even years, in the interim certainly seems a worthwhile objective for policy.

Selected Applications of Happiness Economics

Happiness research has been applied to a range of issues. These include the relationship between income and happiness, inequality and poverty, the effects of macro policies on individual welfare, and the effects of public policies aimed at controlling addictive substances. As is noted above, happiness surveys are particularly well suited to addressing questions that revealed preferences do not answer well.

Some studies have attempted to separate the effects of income from those of other endogenous factors, such as satisfaction in the workplace. Studies of unexpected lottery gains find that these isolated gains have positive effects on happiness, although it is not clear that they are of a lasting nature (Gardner and Oswald, 2001). Other studies have explored the reverse direction of causality, and find that people with higher happiness levels tend to perform better in the labor market and to earn more income in the future (Diener et al., 1993; Graham et al., 2004).

A related question, and one which is still debated in economics, is how income inequality affects individual welfare. Interestingly, the results differ between developed and developing economies. Most studies of the United States and Europe find that inequality has modest or insignificant effects on happiness. The mixed results may reflect the fact that inequality can be a signal of future opportunity and mobility as much as it can be a sign of injustice (Alesina et al., 2004). In contrast, recent research on Latin America finds that inequality is negative for the well-being of the poor and positive for the rich. In a region where inequality is much higher and where public institutions and labor markets are notoriously inefficient, inequality signals persistent disadvantage or advantage rather than opportunity and mobility (Graham and Felton, 2006a).

Happiness surveys also facilitate the measurement of the effects of broader, non-income components of inequality, such as race, gender, and status, all of which seem to be highly significant (Graham and Felton, 2006a). These results find support in work in the health arena, which finds that relative social standing has significant effects on health outcomes (Marmot, 2004).

Happiness research can deepen our understanding of poverty. The set point theory suggests that a destitute peasant can be very happy, while a millionaire can be miserable. (What I call the 'happy peasant' problem is discussed in greater detail in Chapters 4 and 6.) While this contradicts a standard finding in the literature—namely, that poor people are less happy than wealthier people within countries—it is suggestive of the role that low expectations or adaptation to bad circumstances can play in explaining persistent poverty in some cases. The procedural utilities and capabilities approaches, meanwhile, emphasize the constraints on the choices of the poor.

What is perceived to be poverty in one context may not be in another. People who are high up the income ladder can identify themselves as poor, while many of those who are below the objective poverty line do not, because of different expectations (Rojas, 2004). In addition, the well-being of those who have escaped poverty is often undermined by insecurity and the risk of falling back into poverty. Income data do not reveal the vulnerability of these individuals, yet happiness data show that it has strong negative effects on their welfare. Indeed, their reported well-being is often lower than that of the poor (Graham and Pettinato, 2002a).

Happiness surveys can be used to examine the effects of different macro-policy arrangements on well-being. Most studies find that inflation and unemployment have negative effects on happiness. The effects of unemployment are stronger than those of inflation, and hold above and beyond those of forgone income (Di Tella et al., 2001). The standard 'misery index', which assigns equal weight to inflation and unemployment, may be underestimating the effects of the latter on well-being (Frey and Stutzer, 2002b).

Economic growth, meanwhile, can have unexpected effects on happiness. Recent studies based on the Gallup Poll find a 'paradox of unhappy growth', in which growth seems to have a negative effect on happiness (after controlling for individuals' own income).[8] (Lora and Chaparro, forthcoming; Stevenson and Wolfers, 2008). The paradox holds for countries that are above the median income for the worldwide sample, and for countries that are growing faster than the median rate, but not for the poorer, slower growing countries. It is also strongly driven by regional effects, such as rapid

---

[8]   While a number of studies have identified the trends in the data, the term 'the paradox of unhappy growth' is my contribution to the literature.

growth in unhappy countries in Africa and in Russia. One can imagine that rapid growth in countries with such unsettled institutional contexts could be as unsettling as it is necessary. At the micro level, this paradox is mirrored by the contrast between happy peasants and frustrated achievers. In fast-growing developing countries, frustration and unhappiness is often higher for upwardly mobile middle income respondents than it is for the very poor (Graham and Pettinato, 2002a; Knight and Gunatilaka, 2007; Whyte and Hun, 2006). Both of these paradoxes are discussed in detail in Chapter 5.

Political and other institutional arrangements also matter. Much of the literature finds that both trust and freedom have positive effects on happiness (Helliwell, 2003; Layard, 2005). Research based on variance in voting rights across cantons in Switzerland finds that there are positive effects from *participating* in direct democracy (Frey and Stutzer, 2002b). Research in Latin America finds a strong positive correlation between happiness and preference for democracy (Graham and Sukhtankar, 2004). There is some recent research that shows that higher levels of participation in religious organizations—are linked to higher levels of happiness—even for the non-religious respondents that live in those regions (Clark and Lelkes, 2009). These findings hold even when controls for social capital— for example, the extent to which people participate in all sorts of civic organizations—are included. At the same time, *both* sets of variables may be picking unobservable character traits that explain both civic and religious participation.

Finally, people seem to adapt to institutional and other social arrangements that are non-optimal, such as high levels of crime and corruption. In recent work on Latin America with Soumya Chattopadhyay, I find that the higher the generalized crime level or crime norm in a country, the lower the unhappiness effect of being a crime victim. A related study by Cardenas et al. finds that respondents that report having been a victim of crime once in the past year are less happy, on average, than others, but those that report being a victim of more than one crime show no significant negative effects on well-being. Both studies are likely picking up some sort of adaptation to higher levels of crime, as well as the higher stigma that comes from being victimized when crime is a less common event.[9] This is discussed in greater detail in Chapter 6.

Happiness surveys can also be utilized to gauge the welfare effects of various public policies. How does a tax on addictive substances, such as tobacco and alcohol, for example, affect well-being? A recent study on cigarette taxes suggests that the negative financial effects may be outweighed by positive self-control effects (Gruber and Mullainathan, 2002).

Policy Implications

Richard Layard (2005) makes a bold statement about the potential of happiness research to improve people's lives directly via changes in public policy. He highlights the extent to which people's happiness is affected by status—resulting in a rat race approach to work and to income gains, which in the end reduces well-being. He also notes the strong positive role of security in the workplace and in the home, and of the quality of social relationships and trust. He identifies direct implications for fiscal and labor market policy—in the form of taxation on excessive income gains and via re-evaluating the merits of performance-based pay.

---

[9] Cardenas et al. (forthcoming); Graham and Chattopadhyay (2009). For similar evidence on South Africa, see Powdthavee (2005).

While many economists would not agree with Layard's specific recommendations, there is nascent consensus that happiness surveys can serve as an important complementary tool for public policy. Scholars, such as Diener and Seligman (2004) and Kahneman et al. (2004), advocate the creation of national well-being accounts to complement national income accounts, and there are ongoing efforts by the governments of both France and United Kingdom to consider the viability of such indicators. The nation of Bhutan, meanwhile, has introduced the concept of 'gross national happiness' to replace gross national product as a measure of national progress.

Despite the potential contributions that happiness research can make to policy, a note of caution is necessary in directly applying the findings, both because of the potential biases in survey data and because of the difficulties associated with analyzing this kind of data in the absence of controls for unobservable personality traits. In addition, happiness surveys at times yield anomalous results which provide novel insights into human psychology—such as adaptation and coping during economic crises—but do not translate into viable policy recommendations. (This is discussed in Chapter 6.)

One example is the finding that unemployed respondents are happier (or less unhappy) in contexts with higher unemployment rates. The positive effect that reduced stigma has on the well-being of the unemployed seems to outweigh the negative effects of a lower probability of future employment (Clark and Oswald, 1994; Eggers et al.; Stutzer and Lalive, 2004). Indeed, in Russia even *employed* respondents prefer higher regional unemployment rates. Given the dramatic nature of the late 1990s crisis, respondents may adapt their expectations downwards and are less critical of their own situation when others around them are unemployed. One interpretation of these results for policy—raising unemployment rates—would obviously be a mistake. At the same time, the research suggests a new focus on the effects of stigma on the welfare of the unemployed.

In addition, while the lack of definition of happiness is what makes it a survey instrument that can cross countries and cultures without introducing bias, the definition of happiness surely matters to policy. What that definition is—for example, pure contentment or happiness as fulfillment in the more eudemonic Aristotelian sense—entails normative choices that may be very different across countries and cultures. A related challenge is cardinality versus ordinality. Happiness surveys are ordinal in nature, and there is no value attached to a particular score on a ladder or category. Yet from a policy perspective, we may care more about making someone who is truly miserable happier than making an already happy person very happy. Again, these are normative issues that have not been resolved in either the academic literature or in policy debates.

Happiness economics also opens a field of research questions which still need to be addressed. These include the implications of well-being findings for national indicators and economic growth patterns; the effects of happiness on behavior, such as work effort, consumption, and investment; and the effects on political behavior. In the case of the latter, surveys of unhappiness or frustration may be useful for gauging the potential for social unrest in various contexts.

In order to answer many of these questions, researchers need more and better quality well-being data, particularly panel data (as noted above, data which follow the same people over time), which allow for the correction of unobserved personality traits and correlated measurement errors, as well as for better determining the direction of causality (e.g., from contextual variables like income or health to happiness versus the other way around). These are major challenges in most happiness studies. Hopefully, the combination of better data and increased sophistication in econometric techniques will allow economists to better address these questions in the future. In the following chapters of this book, I review some of the contributions that happiness surveys have already made in answering some of these questions—including the continuing debate over the relationship between happiness and income. I also raise some questions that are still unanswered but that can be illuminated by happiness surveys, such as the effects of macroeconomic and political arrangements on happiness and the extent to which individuals adapt to phenomena, such as bad health, crime, corruption, and lack of freedom. I conclude with a discussion of the promises—and pitfalls—of applying the findings from these surveys directly to policy questions.

CHAPTER 2

The Happiness and Income Debate

Substance, Methodology, and the Easterlin Paradox[1]

Will raising the incomes of all increase the happiness of all?
Richard Easterlin (1974)

Happiness economics has increasingly entered the mainstream. Yet, rather ironically, there is much less consensus today than there was in the early stages of happiness research on the first question that it originally shed light on: the relationship between happiness and income. It has become one of the most controversial questions in the discussion of how or if the study of happiness can help economists understand how to enhance welfare or well-being. Does having more money make you happier? And if so, how much more money do you need to be just a little bit happier or very happy?

---

[1] This chapter draws heavily on a paper co-authored with Soumya Chattopadhyay and Mario Picon for an October 2008 Princeton Conference on International Differences in Well Being. The authors would like to thank Peyton Young, Andrew Felton, and Charles Kenny, as well as the participants and reviewers from the Princeton conference for very helpful comments. See Graham et al. (forthcoming).

Richard Easterlin, who was mentioned in the previous chapter, was the first economist to systematically explore the relationship between average country happiness levels and per capita incomes over several decades. His seminal work highlighted an apparent paradox: as countries grew materially wealthier—and healthier—over time: average happiness levels did not increase.[2] His findings are now known as the Easterlin paradox. A number of subsequent studies confirmed the general direction of his findings—for example, average happiness levels do not increase as average incomes increase over time. In contrast, more recent research, based on new data, questions whether the paradox exists at all. Thus there is renewed debate over Easterlin's original question: 'will raising the incomes of all increase the happiness of all?'

Easterlin's paradox has been explained by rising aspirations and comparison effects. Once basic needs are met, aspirations rise as quickly as incomes, and individuals care as much about how they are doing in comparison with their peers as they do about absolute gains. The importance of aspirations and comparison effects to individual well-being has been demonstrated in smaller-scale studies of individual attitudes across a range of contexts from neighborhoods in the United States to cities in Latin America to regions in Russia. These are discussed in greater detail in Chapters 5 and 6.[3] There is also a time dimension: most people think that they were less happy in the past and expect to be happier in the future. They judge their past living standards by their current aspirations, but fail to account for their aspirations adjusting over time as they predict their future happiness.[4]

---

[2] See Easterlin (1974, 2003).

[3] See Graham and Felton (2006a); Kingdon and Knight (2007); Lora and Chaparro (forthcoming); Luttmer (2005).

[4] Easterlin (2001).

Within countries, across cultures and levels of development, Easterlin and a host of other economists have shown that wealthier people are, on average, happier than poorer ones, although the relationship is not necessarily linear, and the additional increases in happiness that come from extra income diminish as absolute levels of income increase (as in the case of the utility function in standard textbook economics). A number of studies show that the same proportional increase in income yields a lower increase in happiness at higher income levels.[5] Differences in income, meanwhile, only account for a low proportion of the differences in happiness among persons, and other economic and non-economic factors, such as employment and health status, exert important influences on happiness. Studies in a wide range of countries, discussed in Chapter 3, demonstrate that the relationship between income and happiness is complex, and is mediated by a number of non-income variables, such as health.

Individual personality differences also play a role, although they are difficult to measure. It may be that those individuals that prize material goods more highly than other things in life are less happy, and thus as ownership of material goods increases (via higher levels of income), happiness levels do not increase proportionately.[6] Finally, there is also some evidence that happier people earn more (and are healthier) than unhappy people.[7]

---

[5] Blanchflower and Oswald (2004); Easterlin (1974, 2003); Frey and Stutzer (2002a); Graham and Pettinato (2002a).

[6] Frey (2008).

[7] This finding holds for people who are, on average, happier, but not necessarily for those that are the happiest in every sample. See Diener and Diener (2008); Graham et al. (2004).

As noted in Chapter 1, there is renewed debate over whether the Easterlin paradox actually exists. A number of scholars, such as Angus Deaton, and Betsey Stevenson and Justin Wolfers, have published papers demonstrating a clear relationship between per capita incomes and average happiness levels, with no sign that the correlation weakens, either as income levels increase or over time.[8] Indeed, the work of both sets of authors suggests that the slope may be steeper for richer countries, most likely because wealthier people are better able to enjoy higher levels of income than are poor ones (a greed effect?).[9] Both of these papers rely on the newly available Gallup World Poll, which covers over 120 countries worldwide, as well as some different data sets for earlier years. Ron Inglehart, meanwhile, in a new analysis of data from the World Values Survey for 1981–2006 finds that subjective well-being rose in 77% of the 52 countries for which data on the same countries over time is available.[10] Eduardo Lora and colleagues at the Inter-American Development Bank, using Gallup data for Latin America, also find a positive relationship between per capita income levels and average happiness levels.[11]

Other studies come out somewhere in the middle. Stefano Pettinato and I, in the first study of happiness in a large sample of developing countries and using absolute levels of per capita gross domestic product (GDP), found that, on average, happiness levels are higher in the developed than in the developing countries in the sample, but that *within* each group of countries,

[8]   Deaton (2008); Stevenson and Wolfers (2008).

[9]   Deaton gets a positive and significant coefficient on a squared specification of the income variable. Stevenson and Wolfers split their sample into those countries above and below $15,000 per capita (in year 2000 US dollars); they get a slightly steeper slope for the rich countries than for the poor ones.

[10]   Inglehart et al. (2008).

[11]   Inter-American Development Bank (2008).

there is no clear income–happiness relationship (see Figure 1.1). Our work is based on the World Values Survey and on the Latinobarometro poll for Latin America.

Why the discrepancy? It is possible that, for a number of reasons, the divergent conclusions may each be correct. The relationship between happiness and income is mediated by a range of factors that can alter its slope and/or functional form. These include the particular questions that are used to measure happiness; the selection of countries that are included in the survey sample; the specification of the income variable (e.g., if absolute levels or a logarithmic specification of income are used; this is discussed in detail below); the rate of change in economic conditions in addition to absolute levels; and changing aspirations as countries go from the ranks of developing to developed economies. I provide evidence from our own analysis of Gallup and Latinobarometro data, as well as from the work of several other authors. My objective is as much to contribute to the method as to the substance of the debate on income and happiness.

Question Framing Issues

Which happiness question is used makes a difference to the relationship between happiness and income. Psychologist Ed Diener and colleagues decompose subjective well-being into an affective or emotional component and a cognitive or judgmental component.[12] The first is determined and measured by how often an individual reports experiencing positive or negative affect (such as smiling), while life satisfaction is composed of

---

[12] Diener et al. (1999).

an individual's satisfaction with various life domains (such as health and work) as well as with life in general. Affect questions typically (and not surprisingly) have less of a relationship with income than do cognitive questions. More framed life satisfaction questions, such as Cantril's ladder of life question, which asks respondents to compare their lives to the best possible life they can imagine on a one to ten scale, have an even closer relationship with income.[13]

The earlier surveys that Easterlin and others used, such as the World Values Survey and the Eurobarometro, relied on open-ended happiness or life satisfaction questions, which posed very simply 'generally speaking, how happy are you with your life?' or 'how satisfied are you with your life?', with possible answers on various scales, ranging from one to four to one to ten. Answers to general happiness and life satisfaction questions are highly correlated.[14] In contrast, the 'life satisfaction' variable that is used in the Gallup World Poll—which is the basis for the Deaton and the Stevenson and Wolfers papers—is Cantril's best possible life question. The best possible life question provides much more of a reference frame than does an open-ended life satisfaction question. Surely when asked to compare their lives to the best possible life, respondents in very poor countries are aware that life is likely better in wealthier ones, not least because of how widely available information has become about how the rich in wealthy countries live, due to widespread access to the media and the internet.

[13] Cantril (1965).
[14] Blanchflower and Oswald find a correlation coefficient of 0.50 for the two questions in Europe and the United States; Graham and Pettinato find one of 0.55 for Latin America, where the questions were used interchangeably in various years of the Latinobarometro poll. Blanchflower and Oswald (2004); Graham and Pettinato (2002a).

Deaton makes a similar point about the Gallup World Poll findings: when asked to imagine the best and worst possible life for themselves on a ten-point scale, people use a global standard, and the Danes understand how bad life in Togo is, and the Togolese, through TV and other media, understand how good life is in high income countries.[15] John Helliwell, meanwhile, compares results based on the Cantril ladder in the 2006 Gallup Poll with those on life satisfaction as a whole in the World Values Survey, and finds that the correlation between income and life satisfaction is stronger with the more framed ladder of life question. At the same time, there is striking consistency in the other factors that contribute to life satisfaction across the two surveys.[16]

As a simple test of the extent to which question framing matters, my colleagues and I compared the income and happiness relationship across several different life satisfaction questions for the Latin American sub-sample of the Gallup World Poll.[17] Latin America is a good testing ground as the region includes countries with a wide range of income levels, with some wealthier countries, such as Chile and Brazil, near OECD levels, and others, such as Guatemala and Honduras, at the other extreme of the development spectrum. The questions included: the best possible life question described above; an economic satisfaction question (are you satisfied with your standard of living, all the things that you can buy and do?); a poor–rich scale question (on a scale from zero to ten, with zero the poorest people and ten the richest people, in which cell would you place yourself?); an affect question (did you smile or laugh a lot yesterday?); a

[15] Deaton (2008).

[16] Helliwell (2008).

[17] The initial results and detail on the methodology for this analysis are in Picon (2008).

life purpose question (do you feel your life has purpose or meaning?)[18]; and a freedom/opportunity question (are you satisfied with your freedom to choose what to do with your life?). (For exact question phrasing and the distribution of responses across questions, see Appendix 2.1.)

Given that accurately measuring incomes in a context such as Latin America is difficult, we used both income and wealth variables. A large percentage of respondents work in the informal sector or in unsteady jobs and have difficulty accurately recalling earnings, for example. And the most recent income levels which are reported may misrepresent more permanent income flows, due to seasonality, economic shocks, and/or job instability. Wealth indices, on the other hand, while adjusting better for temporary fluctuations, are less effective at capturing variability across households, particularly at the high end of the income scale, nor do they account for the quality of assets. Access to water may be irregular, or televisions and refrigerators that are owned may be functioning poorly, if at all.

For our income variable, we used log of per capita household income measured in 2005 purchasing power parity (PPP) US dollars.[19] This

---

[18] This question is slightly problematic, at least in econometric terms, as 96% answer yes to the yes-no question, providing very little variance for analytical purposes.

[19] In each country, Gallup includes a categorical question on total household income. Each respondent is asked to identify the household's monthly income within a bracket expressed in local currency. The number of brackets is different in each country, and in Latin America it ranges from four brackets in Colombia to 20 in Bolivia. We relied on an adjustment to the Gallup income variable introduced by colleagues at the Inter-American Development Bank (IADB). Each household was assigned a normalized random value within the bracket that they self-reported. Income was transformed to US PPP dollars and then divided by household size, resulting in a monthly per capita household income variable which is normally distributed across the sample. The most common adaptation for scale is to divide total household income by the square root of the number of people in the household, under the assumption that there are some economies of scale and children,

specification helps control for outliers, and conforms to standard economic assumptions that an extra unit of income is more significant for those at the bottom of the distribution with less available resources than for those at the top. Some of the earlier studies of income and happiness used absolute rather than log income levels, and show a curvilinear relationship between income and happiness, suggesting the satiation point that is part of the explanation of the Easterlin paradox. Easterlin himself notes that the specification of the income variable has important effects, and that 'the supposed attenuation of the income-happiness relation does not occur when happiness is regressed on log income'.[20] Later studies, such as Stevenson and Wolfers (2008), and Deaton (2008), use either log of average GDP per capita or the average of log income per capita. For our country-level analysis, we used the average log of per capita household income (as opposed to the log of the average per capita household income).[21]

We constructed our wealth index, based on the list of assets in the Gallup Poll.[22] We tested the cross-country relationship between income and

for example, consume less than equivalent adults. The IADB adaptation divided income by the number of household members. As a check, we adjusted the same income variable by the square root of household size and got essentially the same results.

[20] Easterlin (2005).

[21] In theory, these two should be identical. In practice, with substantial misreporting at the top and with a very fat left tail (with far fewer observations on the right/top), the log of the average may place higher relative weight on the households at the bottom of the distribution and smooth out the effects of the outliers on the right.

[22] We used both the simple, unweighted scale of asset ownership, and then a principal components analysis (PCA) based index, in which the assets that are more unequally distributed across households are weighted more. Our results are essentially identical using alternative methods; the results on wealth reported in the tables are those based on the PCA approach. For more detail on the particular assets in the index and its construction, see Graham et al. (forthcoming).

happiness across questions, using happiness as measured by each question as the dependent variable, and then explored how the relationship varied according to average (log of) per capita income in the country and with the typical socio-demographic profile of respondents in each country.[23] We find that the log-linear income and happiness relationship holds across countries for the best possible life and the poor to rich economic ladder questions, but not for affect (smiling a lot the previous day), life purpose, and freedom to choose in life questions. Indeed, the relationship between income and the smiling and life purpose questions is negative and significant when we use our income variable, and insignificant when we use our wealth variable. The relationship of freedom to choose and income (and wealth), meanwhile, is positive, but insignificant.

At the individual level, our basic model was analogous, with happiness as the dependent variable, and then exploring the effects of household wealth, the socio-economic and demographic profiles of respondents, and controls for unobservable traits specific to each country.[24] We found that income and wealth were positively correlated with most measures of happiness except for the life purpose and freedom to choose questions, which were insignificant with some specifications (see Table 2.1). This confirms the work of many other studies, which consistently find a cross-sectional relationship between happiness and income *within* countries, regardless

---

[23] We use the following model: *average happiness (as measured by each separate question) in country i = f (average log of per capita income or wealth in country i + characteristics of the average individual in country i)*.

[24] The model is: *individual happiness = f (household log income or wealth + personal controls + country dummies)*. We ran the model sequentially, first looking at just happiness and income or wealth, then adding the country dummies, and finally adding the personal controls.

Table 2.1 Question phrasing—income and happiness across and within Latin American countries

Subjective variable	Summary of results happiness versus income per capita (yes means significant at the 10% level)					Summary of results happiness questions versus wealth index (yes means significant at the 10% level)				
	Individual cross-sectional analysis			Cross-country analysis		Individual cross-sectional analysis			Cross-country analysis	
	Model 1	Model 2	Model 3	Model 4	Model 5	Model 1	Model 2	Model 3	Model 4	Model 5
Best possible life	Yes (+)	Yes (+)	Yes (+)	Yes (+)	Yes (+)	Yes (+)	Yes (+)	Yes (+)	Yes (+)	Yes (+)
Living standard satisfacction	Yes (+)	Yes (+)	Yes (+)	No (+)	No (+)	Yes (+)	Yes (+)	Yes (+)	Yes (+)	Yes (+)
Place in socio–economic scale	Yes (+)	Yes (+)	Yes (+)	Yes (+)	Yes (+)	Yes (+)	Yes (+)	Yes (+)	Yes (+)	Yes (+)
Life purpose	No (+)	Yes (+)	Yes (+)	Yes (−)	Yes (−)	Yes (+)	Yes (+)	Yes (+)	No (−)	Yes (−)
Smiled	Yes (+)	Yes (+)	Yes (+)	Yes (−)	No (−)	Yes (+)	Yes (+)	Yes (+)	No (−)	Yes (−)
Satisfaction with personal freedom	Yes (+)	Yes (+)	No (+)	No (+)	No (−)	Yes (+)	Yes (+)	Yes (+)	No (+)	No (−)

Model 1: Probit/Oprobit: subjective variable = f(logpcincome)
Model 2: Probit/Oprobit: subjective variable = f(logpcincome), country dummies
Model 3: Probit/Oprobit: subjective variable = f(logpcincome), country dummies, demographics
Model 4: Oprobit country average subjective variable = f(country average hh per capita income)
Model 5: Oprobit country average subjective variable = f(country average hh per capita income, demographics)
Source: Gallup World Poll (2007) and author's calculations.

of whether or not the Easterlin paradox holds across countries or through time.

Across the questions, we find that the highest effect size—based on the size of the coefficients—is between satisfaction with one's standard of living and income (and/or wealth: 0.43 on log income/0.39 on wealth). This is followed by the poor to rich scale economic ladder question (0.32/0.35), and the best possible life question (0.27/0.29). Income and wealth do a good job of explaining the distribution of responses on the ladder of life question, including when other controls are used, but they do not explain answers on smiling, life purpose, and freedom to choose questions. The first three questions provide more of an economic frame for people, while the latter are vaguer and more open ended.

Our results comparing across the questions, both across countries and within them, support our intuition that question framing can have important effects on the measured relationship between income and happiness. Questions that provide more tangible economic or status frames seem to have a closer relationship with income than do more open-ended questions that capture either affect and/or life chances.

One example from our most recent work, which supports this broader point, is from a study we conducted of happiness in Afghanistan (discussed in detail in Chapter 3). Afghans had relatively high mean happiness scores compared to averages for contexts, such as Latin America, where objective conditions are surely better, as well as compared to the world average. Yet their answers on the best possible life question were quite a bit lower than the world average. This suggests that while Afghans may be naturally cheerful, or else have adapted their expectations downwards in the face of very adverse conditions, they are quite realistic as they assess their circumstances in relative terms. Their answers reflect their awareness of how their lives compare to a global reference point for the best possible life (see Chapter 3).

The work of several other scholars supports the basic direction of our findings. Psychologists Ryan and Colleen Howell, using a meta-analysis of 111 samples from 54 developing countries, find evidence of an Easterlin effect: the relationship between income and subjective well-being is stronger for the poor countries than it is for the rich countries in their sample. Yet they also find that the income–subjective well-being relationship is stronger when subjective well-being is measured as life satisfaction than when it is measured as happiness. They describe the former as a more cognitive assessment and the latter as a more emotional assessment.[25]

Jim Harter, also using the Gallup World Poll, finds that different kinds of questions display different results depending on the income levels of the countries. Poor countries slope higher for pain and sadness questions, while rich countries slope higher for enjoyment questions (such as, how often did you smile yesterday?). This likely reflects different concerns at different levels of development. For those for whom basic needs and health are precarious, survival-level issues, such as avoiding pain and death, are paramount, while respondents in wealthier countries, who for the most part take basic needs for granted, have higher expectations about more expansive components of life, such as enjoying leisure time.

These findings echo Deaton's steeper slope on the income–happiness relationship for rich countries than for poor ones. Both sets of findings reflect that respondents in wealthier countries are better able to enjoy income because they are better positioned to use it for a broader range of things other than basic needs (and may have more time to enjoy their

---

[25] Howell and Howell (2008).

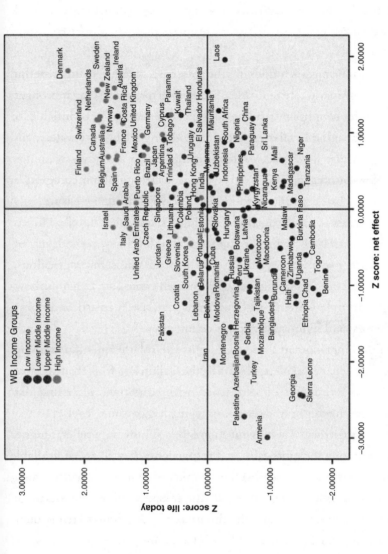

Figure 2.1 Evaluated well-being and net effect

Source: James A. Harter, '*Gallup World Poll: Methodology and Validation*'. Presentation to Gallup Positive Psychology Summit, Washington, DC, October 2008.

incomes as well?). As a result, questions which speak to survival issues seem to be more relevant to respondents in poor countries, while those that speak to enjoyment or quality of life issues resonate more among rich country respondents.

Other possible factors muddying the waters are measurement error and the role of non-market income. Measurement error is a particular problem for developing countries with large informal sectors, as it is difficult for workers with unstable salaries to estimate their earnings accurately, and at the same time, weak tax systems provide strong incentives to under-report. Non-market income, meanwhile, is a factor in both contexts. In rich countries, better public goods and assets which facilitate leisure, such as inherited assets, may contribute to higher happiness levels, but are not directly correlated with per capita income levels. In poor countries, meanwhile, non-market income in the form of subsistence agriculture, home-grown food, and family networks can all contribute to happiness— or mitigating unhappiness—although they are not reported as income. These factors vary significantly across countries.

Work on other domains also highlights the role of question framing. Mauricio Cardenas and colleagues, using the Gallup Poll for Latin America, look at the determinants of satisfaction with education. They find that satisfaction with education does not vary much by income levels, but that it is *negatively* correlated with education levels. This surely reflects higher aspirations among the more educated respondents, as well as less available information (such as test scores) upon which to base assessments among poorer ones. Another explanation for the mixed findings on education, meanwhile, is the extent to which education is endogenous to many other variables which are also correlated with happiness, such as income, social trust, and health.

When they compare satisfaction with life across different education levels, they find that education levels are positively correlated with life satisfaction when a ladder of life question is used, but they are negatively correlated when a satisfaction with standard of living question is used. When they include controls for differences in the innate optimism of individuals, the positive correlation on the ladder question becomes insignificant, while the negative correlation between education satisfaction and satisfaction with standard of living holds.[26] Their findings reflect higher expectations among the more educated, as well as question framing.

Country Selection Issues

Most economists agree that there is some relationship between income and happiness across countries, with wealthier countries generally showing higher levels of happiness than poorer ones. Yet different surveys sample different selections of countries, and that too seems to affect the strength of the relationship, and in part help explain the debate over how strong it is.

My above-mentioned work with Pettinato, based on a large sample of Latin American and OECD countries and an open-ended life satisfaction question, finds a relationship between income levels and happiness, although *within* each of the poor and rich country sets there is no clear pattern (see Figure 1.1). Howell and Howell's meta-analysis finds that the income–subjective well-being relationship is weakest among the wealthiest developing countries in their country sample, and strongest among

[26] They control for individual optimism levels/person fixed effects, to the extent possible in a cross-section, via a principal components analysis of domain satisfactions. See Cardenas et al. (forthcoming).

the poorest and least educated countries. They also find that the effect is strongest when economic status is defined as a stock variable (wealth or assets) rather than as a flow variable (income).[27] Education seems to mediate the income–happiness relationship. The most statistically robust correlation, not surprisingly, is for the least educated respondents in the poorest countries. In contrast, there is very little difference in the strength of the relationship between the most educated respondents in the poor or the rich countries.[28]

The Gallup World Poll clearly contains the largest and most diverse set of countries (in terms of region and development levels) of any of the surveys that have been used to study happiness to date. Yet that presents methodological challenges as well as analytical diversity. A large number of the new countries in the Gallup Poll are small, poor countries in sub-Saharan Africa and/or the transition economies, which have seen the dismantling of existing social welfare systems and dramatic falls in happiness. Thus the steeper sloped income and happiness relationship that appears in research based on these data may not be driven by rising incomes and happiness in the rich countries, but by falling incomes and happiness in a large number of small countries at the bottom of the distribution. A similar point has been made by Easterlin[29] about the sample of countries in the World Values Survey. It is not clear, however, how to resolve the problem of different country selection, and dropping large parts of the sample—for example, the transition economies—in order to retain comparability eliminates some of the most important trends in the global economy in recent decades.

[27] Howell and Howell (2008).

[28] They also find that the effect is stronger for men! Howell and Howell (2008).

[29] Richard Easterlin, remarks at Princeton Conference on International Differences in Well Being; Princeton University, Princeton, New Jersey, October 13–14, 2008.

The transition economies surely have had a distinct experience. Easterlin (2008) examines happiness in Eastern Europe from 1989 to 1998 and finds that life satisfaction followed the V-shaped pattern of GDP for those same years, but failed to recover commensurately. Across domains, increased satisfaction with material standards of living occurred at the same time that satisfaction with work, health, and family life decreased. Disparities across cohorts increased, with the unhappiest respondents being the least educated and those over age 30—not surprisingly, those cohorts that were least able to protect themselves from economic dislocation and take up new opportunities offered by the transition.[30]

Since Easterlin did his work, happiness levels have recovered in at least some of the former Soviet Union (FSU) countries, such as Russia.[31] Whether or not they will recover fully in all of them is an open question. But surely their inclusion in cross-country analysis during a time period when happiness levels were unusually low, as well as the inclusion of a large number of small African economies which are likely to perform poorly for the foreseeable future, will affect the slope of the cross-country income and happiness relationship.

Conclusions

Our aim in this chapter was to help disentangle the debate on the Easterlin paradox and, more generally, the income–happiness relationship, both within and across countries. In doing so, we highlight some of the methodological issues and challenges that are germane to both this debate and to the happiness literature more broadly.

[30] Easterlin (2008).
[31] See Eggers et al. (2006).

Our review, based on some of our work and that of many others, finds that while in general rich countries are happier than poor ones, there is a great deal of variance among the countries within the rich and poor clusters, as well as in the slope of the relationship. The results are quite sensitive to the method selected, the choice of micro or macro data, and the way that happiness questions are framed, thus supporting divergent conclusions about the importance of the paradox.

We find, for example, that question framing makes a major difference to the relationship, in terms of both direction and slope. Analysis based on questions that are framed in economic or status terms, for example, seems much more likely to yield a positive and linear relationship between income and happiness, across and within countries, than are open-ended happiness or affect questions.

Which countries are in the sample also matters. Respondents in poorer countries, who are still struggling to meet basic needs, display a stronger income–well-being link than do those in wealthy countries, where that relationship is mediated by factors, such as relative differences and rising aspirations. Education levels may also mediate that difference, with the least educated respondents in poor countries demonstrating the steepest slope, but more educated respondents in both rich and poor countries having a similar one. There is some evidence, based on the Gallup/Cantril ladder of life question, suggesting that the slope of the income–happiness relationship is steepest at the top of the country wealth distribution, where respondents are either better positioned to enjoy wealth and/or are more aware of how their lives compare to those of others in poor countries. It is not clear that the same steep slope would hold with a more open-ended life satisfaction or affect question.

An additional question is the extent to which the strong income–happiness relationship in more recent work based on the Gallup Poll is driven by falling GDP per capita, driving happiness levels down in a large number of small, poor countries in sub-Saharan Africa, as well as in the turbulent transition economies. This is distinct from rising incomes driving rising happiness levels in the wealthier countries. There is some evidence that both factors may be at play.

A number of paradoxes in the data support our basic propositions, and are discussed in detail in the following chapters of the book. The paradox of unhappy growth, for example, suggests that the rate of change matters as much to happiness as do per capita income levels, and that rapid growth with the accompanying dislocation may undermine the positive effects of higher income levels, at least in the short term. The number of countries experiencing these kinds of changes at the time a survey is conducted could surely affect results. A mirror image of this paradox at the micro level—the happy peasant and frustrated achiever phenomenon—again suggests that the nature and pattern of economic growth, and in particular instability and inequality issues—can counterbalance the positive effects of higher income levels for a significant number of respondents. Finally, low aspirations among the poorest respondents in the poorest countries can bias their responses upwards on a number of questions, particularly those that are more personal and open ended, such as health satisfaction and open-ended happiness questions. The issue of low aspirations and the expectations of the poor in the health and education domains is discussed in detail in Chapter 6.

The income–happiness relationship is also mediated by factors such as inequality levels and institutional arrangements, particularly as countries get beyond the basic needs level. Norms and aspirations are at play, as citizens of particular countries adapt not only to the benefits (and possibly some of the negative externalities) associated with rising incomes, but also to the costs and complexities of things like rising crime and corruption. There is also significant evidence of adaptation to better and more widely available health care, and of an 'Easterlin paradox' in the relationship between happiness and health. These issues are discussed in detail in Chapters 4, 5, and 6.

The complexity of the relationship between happiness and income—and the range of other mediating factors—seems to increase as countries go up the development ladder. Rising aspirations and increasing knowledge and awareness interact with pre-existing cultural and normative differences, as well as the extent and quality of public goods, which are in turn endogenous to the cultural and normative differences. At the same time, because global information and access to a range of technologies are now available to countries at much lower levels of per capita income than was previously the case, they have access to the benefits associated with higher income levels, such as better health care, quite early on in the development process. These complexities, coupled with different conceptualizations of happiness, which are captured differently by the various questions that are used to measure happiness, as well as important differences in the sampling of countries that are studied, are alone sufficient to explain divergent conclusions about the Easterlin paradox.

This chapter has not resolved the debate over whether an Easterlin paradox exists or not. Nor did it intend to. It demonstrated the method-ological and empirical complexities entailed in resolving the debate, as well as in understanding the deeper relationship that it speaks to. In doing so, it also highlights one of the more fundamental contributions of happiness economics: exposing the deep complexities of the determinants of human welfare and the limits to which those determinants can be captured simply via a specification of the income variable. Perhaps they can; perhaps they cannot. The extensive debate on the matter at the least suggests that the answer is surely not as simple as happiness = income, log or linear. What is most notable is the remarkable consistency in the determinants of individual happiness *within* countries of diverse income levels and, at the same time, how happiness is affected by *cross-country* differences that are not directly related to income levels, such as political freedom, the distribution of public goods, and social capital, among others. Income surely plays a role in determining both individual and country-level happiness. Still, assessing its role relative to other more difficult to measure factors will remain a challenge for the foreseeable future, not least because countries at much lower levels of economic development are gaining access to welfare-enhancing goods—for example, information and health technology—something that was unimaginable for the OECD economies when they were at similar per capita income levels many decades ago. The income–happiness relationship may be evolving over time in a manner that we are not yet able to fully comprehend.

Appendix 2.1

Table 2.A.1 Question wording differences in the survey questionnaires

Question on world poll	Type of subjective well-being measured
Did you smile or laugh a lot yesterday?	Affective
Did you feel your life has an important purpose or meaning?	Affective
Are you satisfied or dissatisfied with your income, all the things you can buy and do?	Life-domain satisfaction
Are you satisfied or dissatisfied with your job?	Life-domain satisfaction
Are you satisfied or not with your standard of living, all the things you can buy and do?	Life as a whole satisfaction
Are you satisfied with your freedom to choose what to do with your life?	Life as a whole satisfaction
Please imagine a ladder with steps from zero to ten, if the higher the step, the best possible life, on which step of the ladder do you personally feel you stand?	Life as a whole satisfaction, in relation to others
In a scale from zero to ten, with zero the poorest people and ten the richest people, in which cell do you put yourself?	Life as a whole satisfaction, in relation to others
Measure reflecting changes in best possible life ladder question comparing present to five years ago.	Life as a whole satisfaction compared to the past
Measure reflecting changes in best possible life ladder question comparing what is expected in five years to present.	Life as a whole satisfaction expected in the future

Source: Gallup World Poll (2007).

Table 2.A.2 Distribution of responses across questions

Variable	Obs	Average	Std. Dev.
Smiled	18,816	0.82	0.385657
Life purpose	18,786	0.97	0.1724025
Best possible life	18,952	5.83	2.374283
Satisfaction living standards	18,804	0.69	0.4611318
Poor to rich scale	17,982	4.24	1.847543
Freedom	18,519	0.73	0.4430965

Source: Gallup World Poll (2007).

CHAPTER 3

The Determinants of Happiness around the World

The grumbling rich man may well be less happy than the contented peasant, but he does have a higher standard of living than the peasant.

Amartya Sen (1995)

Most of the original studies of happiness, by both economists and psychologists, focused on OECD countries, and in particular the United States and Europe, all of which were countries that had reached a certain level of economic prosperity.[1] This was due to the availability of data as well as an implicit assumption that people in the developing world were too concerned with day-to-day survival to worry about the more ephemeral concept of happiness. My 2002 work on Latin America with Stefano Pettinato was the first to study happiness in a large-scale sample of developing countries. Our findings were notable in that the basic determinants of happiness were very similar to the OECD countries, although most countries in the

---

[1] Blanchflower and Oswald (2004); Diener and Seligman (2004); Easterlin (1974).

sample were at much lower levels of per capita income, and had substantial proportions of their populations living in subsistence-level poverty. Income surely matters to happiness among individuals within countries, but other key variables, such as age, marital and employment status, and health, matter as much (if not more in some instances). Since then, I have studied happiness in a number of other developing and transition economy contexts. Remarkably, those same patterns seem to conform.

As is clear from the research reviewed in Chapter 2, there is surely a relationship between income and happiness across countries, with wealthier countries being, on average, happier than very poor ones. There may also be a relationship over time as very poor countries begin to get wealthier, but the effect diminishes as they move up the wealth curve. But there are also many outliers, with some very poor countries, like Nigeria, reporting extremely high happiness levels, and other very wealthy ones, like Japan, having relatively low levels, which have also fallen during times of remarkable prosperity. And the nature of that relationship is very much influenced by the happiness question that is used, by the countries in the sample, and by the manner in which income is measured.

Comparing average happiness levels across countries is by definition a difficult and imprecise exercise, as the results may be driven by unobservable differences across countries and cultures as well as by objective circumstances such as economic progress, the nature of governments, and the distribution of public goods.[2] The findings on the determinants of

---

[2] Helliwell (2008).

happiness within countries, meanwhile, are more consistent and robust, as large cross-sections and micro-level data allow us to control for a larger number of factors that vary across individuals—such as age, income, gender, marital and employment status, and so on.

Virtually all studies by economists of happiness within countries find that wealthier people are, on average, happier than poorer ones. They also find remarkable consistency in the effects of other variables, such as age (which has a U-shaped relationship with happiness, with the low point being in the mid to late forties), marital status (marriage is good for happiness, for the most part), unemployment (bad for happiness), and health (very important to happiness).[3] (For an example of the age and happiness relationship for Latin America, see Figure 3.1.) The influence of other variables— such as gender, education, and certain kinds of employment status— on happiness varies more, likely due to different gender rights across countries, to different returns to education as countries make structural changes in varying stages of the development process, and to differences in stability or instability of the self-employed and retired, among others. Studies by psychologists, while usually based on smaller-scale samples and grounded in more in-depth questions, have tended to confirm these findings.[4]

Most of these studies focused primarily on the developed economies, however, and it was assumed that, for the most part, developing countries were different, due to their lower GDP levels, their widespread levels of poverty, and to cultural differences. My research, which began in Latin

[3] See, among others, Blanchflower and Oswald (2004); Frey and Stutzer (2002a); Graham and Pettinato 2002a).

[4] For an excellent review, see Diener and Seligman (2004).

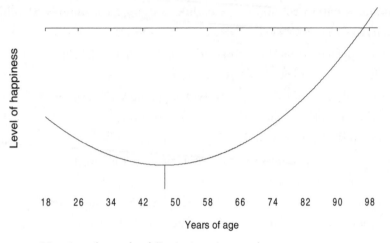

Figure 3.1 Happiness by age level (Latin America, 2000)

America at the beginning of the decade, was the first survey of happiness in a large sample of developing countries. I have since looked at happiness in a wider range of developing or transition economies, ranging from Russia to Central Asia, selected countries in Africa, and Afghanistan. What is most notable about my results, which is supported by the work of Richard Easterlin in the transition economies and by psychologist Robert Biswas-Diener in some of the poorest slums of India, is the extent to which the basic determinants of happiness within countries are the same, regardless of development levels.[5] To the extent that we find modest differences, they are usually easily explained by major structural differences in economies and labor markets and/or by notable changes in those structures faced by countries in transition.

[5] Diener and Biswas-Diener (2008); Easterlin (2008).

THE DETERMINANTS OF HAPPINESS

Comparing Latin America, Russia, and the OECD

Our 2002 study of happiness in Latin America was the first study of happiness in such a large sample of developing countries and certainly the first for the region. We have confirmed the general direction of those findings in a number of studies since then.[6] In the 2002 study, we compared the determinants of happiness in Latin America with those of the United States and Russia. Making such comparisons is fraught with methodological challenges related to both the difficulties of making comparisons across cultures and to the different nature of the data sets that are available. The data we have for Russia, for example, is ideal because it is panel data, data that follows the same respondents over time, interviewing them repeatedly and allowing us to control for individual personality traits or idiosyncrasies. The data for the United States and Latin America is cross-section data—for example, it samples a similar set of respondents each year, but does not follow the same individuals. In both instances, it is possible to gauge trends over time (in the latter by pooling the cross-section data), but the outcome is much more accurate with panel data.

For the United States, we used pooled data for 1973–1998 from the General Social Survey (GSS). We also compared the determinants of happiness in Latin America with those in another large sample of respondents in a very different context, Russia. For Russia, we relied on the most recent available survey (2000) from the Russian Longitudinal Monitoring Survey (RLMS). For Latin America, we relied on the 2001 Latinobarometro. We used 2001 data as it is the one year for which we have variables for both self-reported health status and for being a minority, which makes it comparable

---

[6] Graham and Felton (2006a); Graham and Pettinato (2002a); Graham and Sukhtankar (2004).

Table 3.1 Happiness in the US, 1972–1998

Dependent variable: happiness

Independent variables	Coef.	z
Age	−0.025	−5.20
Age^2	0.038	7.53
Male	−0.199	−6.80
Married	0.775	25.32
Log income	0.163	9.48
Education	0.007	1.49
Black	−0.400	−10.02
Other race	0.049	0.59
Student	0.291	3.63
Retired	0.219	3.93
Housekeeper	0.065	1.66
Unemployed	−0.684	−8.72
Self-employed	0.098	2.29
Health	0.623	35.91
Pseudo R^2	0.075	
Number of obs.	24128	

Note: *Ordered logit estimation; year dummies included but not shown.

Source: GSS data, Author's calculations.

to the United States and Russia surveys. In our other studies, based on a pooled sample of data for several years of Latinobarometro rather than on cross-sections for particular years, we get essentially the same results.

The Latinobarometro (1997–2008) survey consists of approximately 1,000 annual interviews in each of 18 countries in Latin America. The samples are conducted by a prestigious research firm in each country, and are nationally representative, except for Chile, Colombia, and Paraguay.[7] The survey is

[7] Due to logistical and other constraints, the survey only has 70% coverage in Chile; 51% in Colombia; and 30% in Paraguay. The survey is produced by Latinobarometro, a non-profit organization based in Santiago, Chile and directed by Marta Lagos. The first survey was carried out in 1995 and covered eight countries. The data is available, with a

Table 3.2 Happiness in Latin America, 2001
Dependent variable: happiness

Independent variables	Coef.	z
Age	−0.025	−4.21
Age^2	0.000	4.72
Male	−0.002	−0.07
Married	0.056	1.63
Log wealth index	0.395	10.56
Years of education	−0.003	−0.64
Minority	−0.083	−2.49
Student	0.066	1.01
Retired	−0.005	−0.06
Homemaker	−0.053	−1.04
Unemployed	−0.485	−7.54
Self-employed	−0.098	−2.33
Health (self-reported)	0.468	24.58
Pseudo R^2	0.062	
Number of obs.	*15209*	

Note: * Ordered logit estimation; country dummies included but not shown.

Source: Latinobarometro (2001). Author's calculations.

comparable to the Eurobarometer survey for European countries in design and focus; both surveys are cross-sections rather than panels. A standard set of demographic questions is asked every year. The usual problems with accurately measuring income in developing countries where most respondents work in the informal sector and cannot record a fixed salary are present. Many surveys rely on reported expenditures, which tend to be more accurate, if less good at capturing the assets of the very wealthy. The Latinobarometro has neither, and instead relies on the interviewer's assessment of household socio-economic status (SES), as well as a long

time lag, at www.latinobarometro.org. Graham has worked with the survey team for years and assisted with fund-raising, and therefore has access to the data.

Table 3.3 Happiness in Russia, 2000

Dependent variable: happiness

Independent variables	Coef.	z
Age	−0.067	−7.42
Age^2	0.001	7.15
Male	0.152	2.80
Married	0.088	1.40
Log equivalent income	0.389	11.48
Education Level	0.015	0.96
Minority	0.172	2.46
Student	0.199	1.59
Retired	−0.378	−3.97
Housewife	0.049	0.33
Unemployed	−0.657	−6.51
Self-employed	0.537	2.23
Health index	0.446	3.82
Pseudo R^2	0.033	
Number of obs.	5134	

Note: * Ordered logit estimation
Source: Graham et al. (2004).

list of questions about ownership of goods and assets, upon which we compile our wealth index. The index is based on ownership of 11 types of assets, ranging from drinking water and plumbing to computers and second homes.[8]

For Russia, we rely on the Russia Longitudinal Monitoring Survey (RLMS), which covers an average of almost 13,000 Russians per year from 1992 to 2001 and from which we create a panel data set containing data in 1995 and 2000. It is a nationally representative panel study for Russia, carried out in collaboration with the University of North Carolina at Chapel

[8] The correlation coefficient between the interviewer's assessment of SES and our index is 0.50. We also estimated a latent wealth variable using primary component analysis of the items in the wealth index, but this alternative does not substantively change our results.

Hill and with funding from the US Agency for International Development (USAID) among others.[9] For the United States, we use pooled data from the GSS, a nationally representative cross-section survey of approximately 30,000 Americans per year. Our data are for 1973–1998.[10]

We find a remarkable degree of similarity: there are similar age, income, education, marriage, employment, and health effects,[11] see Tables 3.1–3.5. In all contexts, wealthier people are, on average, happier than poorer ones, although the relationship between income and happiness is not necessarily linear. This is not only due to the complex relationship between income and happiness, but also due to the specification of our income variable. We use a logarithmic specification of income in our regressions, which, as is discussed in Chapter 2, attenuates the importance of incomes at the bottom of the scale, where it typically matters more to happiness. There is likely more variance at the top end of the income scale. Education is also positively correlated with happiness in most contexts, except in Latin America, where income and education are so closely correlated that the significance of education goes away when income is included in the regression. Marriage is positively correlated with happiness for the United States (and in Europe, based on other studies), and in Latin America for most years of our survey. Marriage is not, however, significantly correlated with happiness in Russia (where happiness levels are generally lower, and where there has been a

---

[9] More information on the survey can be found at http://www.cpc.unc.edu/projects/rlms/. Critics of the survey question its degree of representativeness. Accepting that some of these criticisms may have validity, we believe it is an extremely valuable data set.

[10] The GSS is publicly available and can be found at: http://www.norc.org/projects/General+Social+Survey.htm.

[11] The coefficient on marriage for Latin America is positive but short of significant for the 2001 sample. For other years for which we have data, the coefficient on marriage is positive and significant.

tumultuous economic transition). Both self-reported health and objective measures of health are positively correlated with happiness in all three contexts.[12]

In all contexts, unemployed people are less happy than others. Self-employed people are happier in the United States and in Russia on average, while in Latin America, they are less happy. While in the United States, self-employment is a choice, in Latin America the self-employed are often in the informal sector by default due to a shortage of stable jobs. The retired are happier than the average in the United States, but much less happy than average in Russia; this confirms many other studies (from very different perspectives) that highlight how poorly Russian pensioners fared in the transition. Another difference is that women are happier than men in the United States, while in Russia men are happier than women (due to disparities in status?) and in Latin America there is no gender difference. Blacks are less happy than other races in the United States, and similarly, those that identify as minorities in Latin America are less happy. In contrast, minorities are happier than ethnic Russians. This is probably because of the increase in status of minorities in post-Communist Russia, and the transition-related losses in income and status for many native Russians.[13]

We cannot establish a direction of causality with these findings. It could be, for example, that health makes people happier or, in turn, that happier people are healthier. Marriage may make people happier; in contrast, happier people may marry each other. We explore causality issues in greater detail at the end of the chapter. Regardless, the consistency in

---

[12] See Graham et al. (2009); Graham and Lora (forthcoming).

[13] These results are discussed in much greater detail in Graham (2005).

the patterns that we find across such very different contexts is remarkable. As we will see below, they hold, for the most part, in even more unusual contexts.

A Bird's Eye View of Happiness in Transition: Central Asia, Cuba, and Eastern Europe

Central Asia is surely a region that has seen its share of changes—and political and economic turmoil—in recent years, and one of the more complex places that I have studied happiness, not least because of political repression and even revolution in some of the countries around the time we were surveying. Working with a team of scholars from the United Nations Development Programme (UNDP) and the World Bank, we implemented a well-being and public opinion survey of four Central Asian countries in October–November 2004. The survey was intended to help identify particular socio-economic and political challenges facing the region. In particular, the analysis focuses on the potential factors that could drive civil unrest in the region, such as economic hardship (both real and perceived) and ethnic tensions; we were also able to include an open-ended happiness question. The survey was implemented in Kazakhstan, Kyrgyzstan, Tajikistan, and Uzbekistan, in collaboration with local polling firms. Surveying in Turkmenistan was not possible due to the complex political situation there. The surveys covered 1,000 respondents per country and were, to the extent possible, nationally representative.

For the most part, we found that the respondents from the surveyed countries are no different from most other populations. Income, as assessed by the respondent's assessment of their purchasing power, and

Table 3.4 Happiness in Central Asia

	Happiness	
	(without country dummies)	(with country dummies)
Urban	−0.0228	−0.0699
Male	0.061	0.1019
Age	−0.0561***	−0.0536***
Age^2	0.0005***	0.0005***
Married	0.4604***	0.403***
Completed technical secondary education	0.1022	−0.0434
Completed regular secondary education	0.0413	−0.0012
Incomplete higher education	0.0447	0.2731*
Complete higher education	0.0253	0.094
Farmer/Dekhan	−0.2068*	−0.0489
Government employee	0.4442	0.3792
Unemployed	−0.4356***	−0.3409***
Socio-economic status	0.4174***	0.4757***
Self-assessed rank	0.4085***	0.452***
Ethnic, self-identified minority	−0.1706*	0.2141*
Kyrgyzstan		−0.1815*
Tajikistan		−0.4726***
Uzbekistan		1.2493***
Pseudo R^2	0.0959***	0.1367***
Observations	5919	5919

Notes: Ordered logistic regression. Dependent variable = 1–4 happiness scale
* Significant at 5% level;   ** Significant at 1% level;   *** Significant at 0.1% level.
Kazakhstan is the left out country dummy.
Source: Graham and Felton (2006b).

socio-economic status, as assessed by the interviewer, are important components of happiness. Perceived socio-economic status and rank also matter to happiness; indeed, statistically, these more subjective variables appear to be even more indicative of someone's happiness than are objective income indicators. This is not a surprise, as perceptions variables tend to correlate more closely with happiness than do most objective ones, as they reflect innate character traits such as optimism—which are shared across response domains.

As in other populations, age has a U-shaped relationship with happiness in Central Asia, although the low point (age 51) is older than that for most OECD economies (usually in the mid-forties) and more typical of the pattern for developing economies.[14] As in the rest of the world, marriage is good for happiness and unemployment is bad for happiness. Higher education, once wealth and status are accounted for, does not have a strong effect on happiness. Health status was, unfortunately, not included in the survey.

While most of the basic patterns are similar, happiness in the region also exhibits some differences from the rest of the world, which likely reflect the rather tumultuous nature of the region's economic and political transition. In particular, a number of aspects of 'social capital' do not seem to follow typical patterns in these countries. Three areas regarding social capital where Central Asia stands out from the rest of the world are trust and community involvement, ethnic relations, and religion.

As in the rest of the world, respondents who say they trust other people, participate in community activities, and feel safe, are happier on average. In Central Asia, however, trusting others is not correlated with happiness. While we cannot explain this in any definitive way, we posit that the authoritarian or semi-authoritarian nature of governments in the region may create a climate of general mistrust (other than at the local level, where

---

[14] Indeed, the happiness–age turning point for most countries in Latin America is identical: 51 years. See Graham and Felton (2006a).

neighbors know each other), and those respondents that report they can trust most individuals are either afraid to report their true sentiments and/or are outliers for other unobservable reasons. Answers to a question about whether the respondent feels safe walking alone at night are significantly correlated with happiness, as one would expect, so this provides additional evidence that the nature and meaning of 'trust' is interpreted differently in Central Asia than in the rest of the world.

Happiness studies also allow us to analyze relations between groups of people, such as ethnic minorities. Migration in the region is high and there is a large contingent of non-Central Asians, Russians in particular. Russians and other ethnic groups that immigrated during the Soviet period, such as Ukrainians, tend to be poorer, older, and less happy than Central Asians. Prior to the fall of communism, Russians tended to have management and other desirable positions; since then, their fate has been much less favorable. Kazakh and Kyrgyz migrants, on the other hand, tend to be wealthier and happier. Looking at the data another way, older migrants (presumably those who migrated before the fall of communism) are much less likely to have an above average economic position than are younger ones, again suggesting that those migrants who are able to take advantage of new economic opportunities have a distinct fate from those who moved in response to pre-transition economic conditions and now have few options.

In terms of reported happiness, we find that outsiders—as defined by their response to a question which combines their non-native origins with whether their ethnicity or their citizenship matters more—as well as by a question about whether they think in the native language—are less happy than others. The only place this does not hold is Kyrgyzstan, where migrants are, on average, happier than others. Minorities in Kyrgyzstan are also outliers, in that their perceived economic rank or position (as measured by the economic ladder question) is higher than average, while for migrants elsewhere it is lower. Finally, migrants or outsiders in Kyrgyzstan are less likely to think that local or national-level conflicts are likely, while elsewhere in the region they are more likely to think conflict is imminent. Those respondents that think conflict is likely are also less happy than others, although the direction of causality is difficult to establish in this instance (in other words, less happy respondents may be more likely to report that conflict and/or other unpleasant events are more likely to occur). In sum, the conditions and outlook of outsiders in Kyrgyzstan seems distinct from that of other migrants in the region. While we do not have definitive evidence, our perspective as surveyors suggests that migration to Kyrgyzstan is more of a response to post-transition economic opportunities than it is in the other countries.

Within Kyrgyzstan, meanwhile, urban residents that live in the south—where the March 2005 rebellion against the Akayev Government began—are no less happy than other respondents, and are indeed less likely to report grievances against the government. This, plus the weak nature of both the government and the leadership of the rebellion, suggests that its outbreak was as much a result of spontaneity as it was a reflection of higher levels of grievance in the south. This demonstrates the need for caution in inferring the propensity for violence and other protest activity (or making any sorts of predictions) from survey data alone.

We also looked at the role of religion. There is a diversity of religions in the region, with 95% of respondents reporting some religious affiliation. In most countries, respondents that express faith or religious affiliation—as well as those who practice their faith—are, on average, happier than others.[15] We attempted to gauge intensity of commitment—and Islamic orientation—by identifying those respondents who prayed five times a day (40% of the sample that responded to the question). In most of the rest of the world, the group with more intense faith would be happier, on average, than others. Instead, the mean happiness scores of the five times a day prayers are almost exactly the same as the average. In contrast, they were more likely to believe they had above average economic status, even though objectively their status, as assessed both by the interviewer and by their response to questions about their purchasing power, tends to be slightly lower than less devout respondents. This may indicate either high levels of optimism, which is not a surprise among the very faithful, or perhaps other types of social status that accrue to religious people in the region.

In general, according to subjective well-being measures, Central Asians are very similar to people around the world. However, the link between happiness and social capital indicators is less strong in the region than it is in most other places—perhaps no surprise for recently independent countries still forging a social contract and for a context where political freedom is incomplete.

Cuba

Cuba is a country that has been at the cusp of economic transition for years, with very minor changes taking place in the structure of its economy, while its political system remains dominated by an authoritarian regime. Yet Cubans have a popular reputation for being remarkably cheerful, given per capita income and the lack of political freedom. The explanation

[15] Clark and Lelkes (2009).

that is usually given is natural cheerfulness among the population and/or widespread access to public health and education services. We do not, however, have reliable, nationwide data for Cuba. Nor do the surveys that exist have an open-ended happiness question that is comparable to the questions in the Latin America, Russia, and US surveys discussed above.

We do have access to a study conducted in the two largest cities in Cuba—Santiago and Havana—by Jesus Rios and Johanna Godoy of the Gallup Organization for the Gallup World Poll, a survey I am also involved in.[16] The study polled 600 respondents in Havana and 400 in Santiago in September, 2006, and compared responses of Cubans to those of other Latin American respondents in the Gallup World Poll for the same year. The results are representative for the 3 million respondents for those two cities, but not beyond. The study was conducted by Gallup without permission of the government, and plans to follow-up that study with a nationally representative sample in late 2007 were put aside after those conducting the pilot interviews were arrested and detained by the police. Thus the results reported here are, as described above, a snapshot, bird's-eye view, and they are limited to urban areas only. Regardless, they are illustrative. The interviews were conducted in person, door to door, and household selection was based on standard, random sampling methods, based on an assessed probability that a particular household selected from a larger sample of households is representative. Interviews were conducted by university students who reside in Cuba, but who were trained by Gallup.

[16] This section is based on Rios and Godoy (2007).

Despite the reputation of Cuba as a happy country, only 62% of Cubans said that they laughed or smiled the day before, as opposed to 82% for Latin America overall, and 64% said that they had experienced enjoyment for much of the previous day, as opposed to 79% for Latin Americans in general. While there is no difference in the percentage of respondents that report negative emotions (such as depression) compared with the Latin American average, there is clearly less positive emotion than is typical for Latin America.

The above set of questions captures positive emotion or 'affect'. Other questions are better suited to capturing different elements of life satisfaction, and on this front, Cubans were more optimistic than the Latin American average about the quality of their public services, but far less positive than the average about their freedom and opportunities to determine their economic welfare. Ninety-six percent of Cubans said that health care was available to anyone, regardless of their economic situation, while 98% say the same about education. The Latin American averages, in contrast, were 42% and 52% respectively. Seventy-eight percent of Cubans were satisfied with the country's schools, as opposed to 59% for Latin America. Satisfaction on the health front, on the other hand, was closer to the regional average: 60% were satisfied with the quality of health services, as opposed to the regional average of 57%. Seventy-six percent of urban Cuban respondents were satisfied with their personal health, as opposed to 85% of urban Latin Americans.

In contrast, Cubans scored much lower than the average on economic opportunity questions. Only 60% of Cubans who have a job say they have the opportunity to do what they do best at work, as opposed to 84% for the region as a whole, and job satisfaction was also lower: 68% were satisfied with their jobs, as opposed to 83% for the region. Only 55% of Cubans reported having had the opportunity to decide what to do with their time the day before, as opposed to 75% of Latin Americans. And, most notably, only 26% of Cubans are satisfied with their freedom to choose what to do with their lives, which is three times lower than the Latin American average of 80%, and is also lower than the scores for Zimbabwe (32%), Chad (31%), and Ethiopia (30%).

The results point to a mixed picture on the well-being front. Cubans have less positive affect than their regional counterparts, which suggests that they might also score lower on an open-ended happiness question if it were available. The results on economic opportunities and freedoms would also likely correlate with lower levels of happiness, and would surely correlate with lower scores on a ladder of life question, such as the Cantril question that is used in the broader Gallup World Poll. At the same time, Cubans are aware that they have good access to public services and are, for the most part, fairly satisfied with the quality of those services, even if they do not seem to translate into economic opportunities.

As in the case of the Central Asian findings, the divergences from the average in Cuban well-being responses seem to be grounded in realistic assessments of what life is like in Cuba, rather than in a nationally shared character trait. At the same time, as we cannot systematically compare Cuban happiness or ladder of life responses to other Latin Americans or to the rest of the world, both because the questions differ and because the Cuban responses are urban only, we must be very cautious about inferring too much from any comparisons.

It is worth thinking about the findings in Cuba in light of Richard Easterlin's (2008) findings for the transition economies of Eastern Europe, which have made much more of a transition to the market economy than Cuba has, but where the availability of public services deteriorated at the same time.[17] Easterlin finds that life satisfaction in the transition economies from 1989 to 1999 followed the same V-shape pattern that GDP did in those countries, but failed to recover commensurately. In general, *increased* satisfaction with material living levels has occurred at the expense of *decreased* satisfaction with work, health, and family life. The disparities in life satisfaction were greatest for the less educated and persons over the age of 30; in both instances, cohorts that were less able than the average to cope with the dramatic transition. In this instance, life satisfaction in different domains reflects the increase in economic opportunity that accompanied the economic transition in Eastern Europe, on the one hand, and the increase in insecurity on the other. The findings are, roughly speaking, the analogue of those for Cuba, where transition has yet to take place.

'Happiness' in Africa[18]

There is very limited data for Africa, both in terms of country coverage and in terms of specific happiness questions in the data that we do have— the Afrobarometer opinion survey, a 'sister' survey to the Latino and Eurobarometers. Still, our exploration of the Afrobarometer data gave us some insights into optimism and other public attitudes on the continent, and how they differ from other developing regions.

As is discussed above and also later in this chapter, our work on optimism and well-being in Latin America and Russia finds that higher levels of optimism and happiness (variables which correlate very closely with

[17] Easterlin (2008).
[18] This section draws heavily on Graham and Hoover (2007).

each other) are also associated with other positive traits and behaviors, such as productivity in the labor market, better health outcomes, and higher levels of support for democracy and markets. Matthew Hoover and I used these findings as a benchmark for our look at Africa. We compare them to new survey data for several countries in Africa, a context where poverty is more widespread and democratic governments and market economies are, for the most part, very fragile, in an attempt to understand these relationships in conditions of extreme adversity. In the absence of a straightforward happiness question, we chose to focus on optimism in Africa.

In most other contexts where we have worked, happiness and optimism are very closely correlated. Our research on happiness in Latin America and Russia (discussed above) finds that happiness and positive expectations for the future are positively correlated, and in turn they are both correlated with support for markets and for democracy (Chapter 7). In work on panel data for Russia (Chapter 4), we find that happiness and optimism about the future are correlated with better outcomes in the labor market and health arenas. Related work by Manju Puri and David Robinson on US data has linked optimism—defined as respondents predicting a longer life expectancy than would be predicted by objective variables, such as parents' longevity and individuals' income, education, and health status—to better financial outcomes, higher risk taking, and higher likelihood of re-marriage, conditional on divorce.[19]

We relied on analogous discrepancies between expected and/or perceived economic status and objective status measures as the basis for assessing optimism in Africa. Our initial results yield notably different patterns

---

[19] Puri and Robinson (2005).

from those we have established in other countries. In Latin America, Russia, and the United States, we find that optimism—defined as positive expectations for the future (for respondents and for their children) and as assessing one's economic status more positively than objective measures do—is highly correlated with *higher* levels of income, better self-reported health, and higher levels of reported well-being in general. In contrast, in Africa, optimism—at least as defined as positive expectations for one's children—and income are *inversely* correlated. Optimism thus defined is also inversely correlated with a number of other indicators of higher standards of living, such as better health status and security from crime, and positively correlated with a number of variables associated with deep poverty.

Given the deep and persistent levels of poverty in Africa, we hypothesize that the explanation lies in human psychology as much as in economic, social, or cultural explanations. We posit that given such extreme conditions, optimism among the poor may be a result of selection bias: individuals in such conditions may have to be optimistic to survive. While we cannot fully test this hypothesis, not least because we do not have over time data on the same respondents, our initial results are certainly suggestive. Alternatively, our results may reflect these individuals' realistic assessment that conditions are so bad they can only improve.

We used the Afrobarometer, a relatively new survey which is modeled on the Euro and Latino Barometers, and carried out with the collaboration of those survey teams and the Michigan State University, the Institute for Democracy in South Africa (IDASA), and the Center for Democratic Development, among others. The survey was first conducted in 1999 (however, the first survey included different questions and covered only five countries). The second round, conducted in 2002 and 2003, included countries as of the time of our research: Cape Verde, Kenya, Lesotho, Malawi, Mali, Mozambique, Namibia, Nigeria, South Africa, Tanzania, and Uganda. At this juncture, the surveys had been carried out in one year per country.

The Afrobarometer interviews between 1,200 and 2,400 individuals from each nation, and includes standard socio-demographic questions: age, education, gender, race, religion, and employment status. The survey includes both an interviewer's assessment of the respondent's socio-economic status, as well as a question which asks respondents to place themselves in one of income categories (in the respondent's local currency), rather than estimating a precise amount of earned income. The income data must be used with caution, given the difficulties of accurately estimating income flows in a context characterized by seasonal variation in employment and a large proportion of the population that works in the informal or black economy.

As noted above, while the Afrobarometer does not have a happiness question, there are a number of questions about perceptions of past, current, and future economic status, as well as about respondents' living standards compared to their children and to their parents, which allow us to assess optimism, if not happiness. There is an economic ladder question (as in the Latinobarometro), which asks respondents to rank themselves on a step ladder representing their society, where the poor are on the first step and the rich are on the tenth. In our previous research, the economic ladder question has proven to be a useful proxy for respondents' views of their relative position in society.

Optimism about future mobility in Latin America, a variable that we call prospects of upward mobility or POUM, is positively correlated with happiness (simple correlation coefficient of 0.14). Respondents' optimism about their children's future mobility—as assessed by a question which asks respondents 'how do you think your children will live compared to you: worse, the same, better?'—is also positively correlated with happiness (0.11). Both kinds of optimism are correlated with higher levels of wealth and education, and with better self-reported health.

For Africa, we focused on the variables that we could use to gauge optimism. We relied on a number of questions which explore respondents' views about their current standard of living and about their achieved and expected income mobility—variables which typically correlate quite closely with happiness. These are phrased: 'how do you live today?', with answers on a five-point scale ranging from very bad to very good; and 'how will you live months from now compared to today?', with answers ranging from much worse to much better.

We do not have a direct question about how respondents think their children will live in comparison to themselves. However, the economic ladder question (ELQ) asks respondents to rank, in turn, themselves, their parents, and their children on their society's economic ladder. We created a change in economic ladder variable (change in ELQ) that subtracted the respondent's score from that of their children, with the intuition being that what mattered was the gap: how much better did the respondents think their children would do. Subtracting the respondent's score from the children's ELQ 'controls' for the individual's own rank isolates, to the extent it is possible, respondents' subjective hopes for their children's future. As the children's ELQ variable is inherently more speculative than the respondents' own score, which is based on more objective information, and we subtract that out, we assume (perhaps somewhat heroically) that it is capturing elements of optimism which are based in character traits rather than in objective circumstances.

THE DETERMINANTS OF HAPPINESS

We found that African respondents' views about their *own* economic situation improving in the near future were positively correlated with income, education, and other variables which are indicative of better socio-economic status, as they are in Latin America. In contrast, we found that the *poorest* respondents in Africa were the most optimistic about their *children's* future mobility. We posit that optimism about the short-term future (months hence) is more closely linked to respondents' objective conditions, such as income and education, and realistic prospects, while assessing one's children's future status compared to one's own is a much more speculative exercise which likely captures innate optimism in addition to objective criteria.

We repeated essentially identical equations for Latin America, based on Latinobarometro data. The results for Latin America ran in the opposite direction from those in Africa—income was *positively* correlated with optimism for children's future.

Given our doubts about accurate income reporting, we assessed poverty in a number of different ways: low reported income category, low levels of education, lack of access to health care, and higher likelihood of being a crime victim. Most of these measures were significantly and positively correlated with reported prospects for children's mobility. For example, respondents who reported that they had been a victim of a crime in the past year were more likely than the average to assess their children's future prospects for mobility positively.[20]

---

[20] One possibility, of course, is that the results are an artifact of construction: those that assessed their own status at the highest level could have, at best, a zero response even if they assessed their children at the highest level, and would have a negative response if they assessed their children's level lower than their own. In order to ensure that our results were not skewed by these responses, we reran the regressions

Table 3.5 Poverty and optimism in Africa and Latin America

Regression of Change_ELQ_Kids in Africa				Regression of Change_ELQ_Kids in Latin America		
Observations	14437			Observation	14279	
LRchi^2(30)	1751.59			LRchi^2(30)	552.69	
Prob > chi^2	0.00			Prob > chi^2	0.00	
Pseudo R^2	0.03			Pseudo R^2	0.01	

Change_ELQ_Kids	Coefficient	T-Score		Change_ELQ_Kids	Coefficient	T-Score
Age	−0.0010	−0.20		Age	−0.0245***	−4.75
Age^2	−0.0000	−0.16		Age^2	0.0001***	3.39
Yeduc	−0.0250***	−2.90		Yedu	0.0049	1.21
Income	−0.0157**	−2.55		*Wealth*	*0.0154**	2.07
Urban	−0.0055	−0.16		Unemp	0.1465**	2.26
Unemployed	0.0093	0.27		Crime_Victim	−0.037	−1.12
Freq_Crime_Victim	0.0272***	2.12		Argentina	0.9390***	5.05
Capeverde	0.9281***	13.27		Bolivia	0.5967***	3.19
Kenya	1.0961***	18.57		Brazil	0.6956***	3.68
Lesotho	−0.7496***	−9.98		Chile	0.9526***	5.15
Mali	0.7510***	10.21		Colombia	0.0596	−0.32
Mozambique	0.4465***	5.86		Costa_Rica	0.3296*	1.76
Malawi	−0.1720**	−2.11		Ecuador	0.0351	0.19
Namibia	0.5072***	7.76		El_Salvador	0.1685	0.90
Nigeria	1.4786***	26.81		Guatemala	0.1505	0.80
S Africa	0.2524***	−3.52		Honduras	0.5891***	3.14
Tanzania	0.6849***	11.54		Mexico	0.6732***	3.61
				Nicaragua	0.0674	0.36
				Panama	0.3858**	2.05
				Paraguay	0.4100**	2.12
				Peru	0.6248***	3.32
				Venezuela	0.4272**	1.98

Notes: Uganda is the dropped country dummy. Latinobarometro (2000).

* Significant at the 10% level.
** Significant at the 5% level.
*** Significant at the 1% level.

THE DETERMINANTS OF HAPPINESS

While our findings are exploratory at best, they suggest that optimism, poverty, and insecurity are inversely correlated in Africa. While we cannot establish causality, we posit that these traits may enhance the survival prospects of the poor in such adverse circumstances, and may help explain how the unusual levels of optimism among the poorest and most insecure respondents depart from findings for more developed regions, where we find that optimism is positively correlated with wealth, education, and other signs of prosperity. The results may also reflect realism on the part of the rich. In the unstable, low growth reality of most African countries, those in the top quintiles would be making realistic assessments that things were not likely to get materially better any time soon, and that their children were not likely to live better than they were.

Future research, hopefully based on panel data which allows us to control for individual specific character traits, is necessary to test whether optimism per se (that which is not explained by objective circumstances) plays a role in helping the poorest survive in Africa, or whether it merely reflects the ability of individuals to adjust their own expectations downward in adverse circumstances, but maintain hope for better lives for their children. These two traits, of course, may be intertwined.

based on a Tobit model where optimism is a latent variable that is reflected in the gap, but truncated at zero and ten. This specification drops all of the responses that are below zero. Most of these below zero responses—7.6% of all of our observations—were respondents in the highest income brackets assessing their children's prospects lower than their own, while an insignificant fraction were at the lower end of the scale (poor respondents assessing their children low or even lower than they). Yet our results were essentially unchanged with this specification. Detailed regression results are available from the authors.

Happiness in Afghanistan: Insights on Human Well-Being in the midst of Turmoil

Similar to Africa, Afghanistan is a context where individuals have to cope with the most adverse of circumstances. Our results once again demonstrate the remarkable consistency across individuals in the determinants of happiness—even in the midst of extreme circumstances. At the same time, relatively high average happiness scores in Afghanistan are balanced by much lower scores on the best possible life question. This suggests that Afghans may be naturally cheerful and/or may have adapted their expectations downwards in the face of adversity, yet at the same time are more realistic—or pessimistic—when thinking about their situation in relative terms.

Our survey of well-being in Afghanistan was made possible by financial support from the Norwegian Government, and was carried out in collaboration with AIRConsulting in Kabul—directed by Ahmad Rahmani, a doctoral fellow at the Rand Corporation, in collaboration with the University of Kabul. We interviewed 2,000 individuals from eight provinces in Afghanistan in January 2009. The interviews were conducted by recent graduates from the university who had received prior training in survey research through a number of international institutions. The survey was intended as a pilot, and the results are by definition preliminary.

Provinces were chosen on the basis of feasibility of conducting interviews, including ability to reach them in difficult winter conditions and the safety of the interviewers. Thus our results come with a caveat, as we have not surveyed in the most difficult and conflict-ridden parts of the country. Still, approximately 400 of our respondents were from areas that were somewhat influenced by the Taliban.

74

THE DETERMINANTS OF HAPPINESS

Within the provinces, individuals were drawn randomly from the whole population. Distribution of samples over the provinces was according to the general population of each province. For example, 1,000 sample points were drawn from the capital, Kabul City; 260 from the next largest city of the north, Mazar-e-Sharif; 40 samples from Aibak (the center of Samangan province); 100 samples from Pol-e-Khomri (the center of Baghlan province); 100 samples from Kunduz city (the center of Kunduz province); 100 samples from the city of Charikar (the center of Parwan province); 300 samples from the city of Jalalabad (the center of Nangarhar province); and finally, 100 samples from Jaghuri district (one of the largest districts of Ghazni province). While sampling was stratified over province and weighted according to the distribution of population in each province, systematic random sampling was used to draw respondents from the lists of general population provided by Afghanistan's Central Statistics Office (ACSO).

Afghan cities are divided into small districts called 'Nahya', each with its own district administrative offices, which maintain reasonably accurate residential lists for their districts. These district administrators report directly to the city municipality; the Nahya is considered to be the lowest unit of aggregation for demographic information. These district offices were kept operational even during the Taliban regime, although they put a religious leader in charge of day-to-day supervision of their work.

An example of the selection process comes from Kabul City, where 1,000 of the 2,000 questionnaires were allocated (its population equals the total population of the other seven cities that were sampled). The 1,000 were then divided into 17 districts of Kabul city, weighted by the total population of each district. A total of that number of samples was drawn from the lists of population by simple systematic random sampling method.[21] The full survey was completed over the course of one month (January 2009).

The team encountered some difficulties in conducting the interviews. During the preliminary testing of the questionnaire, respondents were reluctant to the spend the 40 to 60 minutes required to complete the questionnaire. As a result, we began to offer a modest compensation ($15 in large cities, $8 in small ones) in return for completing the questionnaire. The non-response rate dropped from over 70% to 1.6%.

Other challenges reflect the Afghan context. For example, despite the interviewers' explanation of the survey's purpose, most respondents were skeptical about the intentions. This is not surprising given the complex political situation—and trajectory—in Afghanistan. They were particularly skeptical that such a survey could ever have a positive impact on their personal lives. The interviewers noted that while Afghans are frequently exposed to similar surveys by different institutions, they remain uncomfortable expressing their personal opinions, and tend to give generic responses.

---

[21] Systematic sampling was based on the rule of $K = N/n$, where K = the constant number between two names on the list, N = total population of each district, and n = number of samples allocated for that district. Usually the first number was drawn randomly between 1 to 9 and then the rest of the samples were chosen according to $P2 = P1 + K$, $P3 = P2 + 2K$, $P4 = P3 + 3K, \ldots$, and so on. For district number one of Kabul city, for example, 65,900 people were listed by the district office, a total of 26 samples were allocated to account for the whole population, and then the above formula was applied to account for the rest of the sampling. In some cases where lists were not available, some individuals were chosen completely randomly on the street. However, in most cities the lists were available and the systematic random sampling method was used.

Gender issues were, not surprisingly, also a challenge. Many of the randomly selected women in the survey would not answer the questionnaire (and this was particularly notable in the Taliban-influenced areas). They were typically afraid that their husbands, fathers, brothers, and other relatives would see them talking to a group of strangers. The randomly drawn women in Kabul were much more likely to answer the interviewers than were those interviewed elsewhere. This creates a selection bias in our gender findings, of course, as those who answered were likely much freer and more educated than the average. Cold weather, winter, and snowy roads also created obstacles to the survey process and to interviews on the streets. In a few cases, the team faced serious dangers on mountainous highways in Afghanistan. Finally, insecurity in some areas and towns also made interviewing much more difficult than is typical for such surveys.

Accepting these obstacles and the margin of error that they introduce, our results show surprising consistency with those of happiness surveys in other contexts. Overall, mean happiness levels in Afghanistan, as measured by a general 'how happy are you with your life question?', with the answers ranging from not at all to very (phrased and scaled exactly as in the Latinobarometro), are relatively high. The mean happiness in Afghanistan was 2.62; for Latin America for 1997–2007 (the latest year for which we have data) it was 2.8. The standard deviation in Latin America was higher (0.93 versus 0.91), though, suggesting that there is more variance across countries there than there is across provinces in Afghanistan. Meanwhile, happiness in Latin America in 1997 and 2000 was quite a bit lower than in Afghanistan today (2.35 and 2.36 respectively).[22] The difference in happiness scores across

---

[22] Author's calculations based on the Latinobarometro survey, 1997–2007.

these two contexts is surely much smaller than the difference in objective conditions.

Mean scores on the best possible life question, meanwhile, were quite a bit lower in Afghanistan than in Latin America (although, not surprisingly, respondents with higher scores on the best possible life question were happier than the average). The mean score on the best possible life question was 4.67 on a one to ten scale (with a standard deviation—which is a measure of how far scores depart from the average—of 2.12). The mean score on best possible life for Latin America in 2007 was 5.8 (with a standard deviation of 2.3). The mean for the world (the 129 countries in the Gallup World Poll) was 5.42 (with a standard deviation of 2.18).[23]

These findings suggest that Afghans might be naturally cheerful people (or have adapted their expectations downwards in the face of poor conditions), but when asked to assess their situation in relative or framed terms, they are well aware that they do not have the best possible lives. Their optimism in the face of adversity may be similar to the optimism of the poor in Africa—a need to maintain hope in the face of deep difficulties. At the same time, they are realistic in terms of how their situation compares to the rest of the world. In addition to being an example of downward adaptation (which is discussed in detail in Chapter 5), this also drums home the point on differences in how respondents answer well-being surveys when the frames are different, as is discussed in Chapter 2.

At the individual level, Afghans seem to conform, for the most part, to the usual happiness patterns that hold worldwide. There is a U-shaped age curve, with the turning point being 40 years of age. This is a bit younger than that for the United States, Europe, and for Latin America. Men are happier

---

[23] Author's calculations based on the Gallup World Poll.

than women, which is not surprising given the conditions for women in Afghanistan. Yet the difference is not that great and is only significant at the 10% level. It is likely a result of the selection bias noted above. Because of women's reluctance to answer the survey, they made up 11% of the total respondents in the sample. One can imagine that the women who were willing to take initiative to answer the survey—many of whom were in a university setting—were likely more educated and had more control over their lives than the average in Afghanistan. Married respondents, meanwhile, were not happier than the average. This is a domain in which Afghanistan more closely resembles Russia than the OECD. Both marriage and gender findings must be taken with a grain of salt given the over-representation of men in the sample. Unemployed people (roughly 10% of the sample) were less happy than the average, not significantly which contrasts with most other places in the world and reflects the unusual nature of economic activity in Afghanistan.

The relationship between happiness and income across individuals is remarkably consistent across most countries, with wealthier people being, on average, happier than poor ones. Accurately measuring income in a context such as Afghanistan, however, is difficult, if not impossible. There is a very large informal and underground economy, a significant part of society relies on subsistence agriculture, and there are tremendous incentives for under-reporting of incomes, given both the illicit drug trade and high levels of corruption at all levels of government. Given these constraints, we chose to rely on two kinds of indicators as proxies in our regressions.

The first is an asset index based on reported ownership of 18 assets listed in the survey, with possible answers being yes/no. These assets ranged from sewage, running water, and electricity, to fixed phone lines and computers, to washing machines and vacation homes. Trying to simplify based on asset ownership yielded its own challenges in the Afghan context. For example, only 913 people have electricity, yet a high number of these—787—possess a computer. Even more puzzling, while only 279 people possess running water, 737 of them say they have washing machines. And a very high number—1,787—report having fixed phones. Part of this is explained by the availability of cheap Chinese generators—which substitute for electric service—and by water pumps (411 respondents owned them) substituting for running water. Meanwhile, a large number of people own cell phones and tap into areas where there is coverage, even if they do not have phone plans. Despite these conundrums, there is some normalcy in the distribution: only 142 respondents have vacation homes, while 1,820 have radios and 1,733 have televisions, and 690 have either water pumps or running water, for example. The distribution of assets across the sample, meanwhile, displays a fairly normal curve, meanwhile.

Our second proxy for income is the respondent's own assessment of their economic situation and prospects. The first is the economic ladder question which has been used in many surveys and asks the respondent to place themselves on a ten-step economic ladder representing their society. The second asks the respondent whether the economy is going forward, stalling, or going backwards. As these are perceptions-based measure and responses are influenced by individual character traits (such as happiness), there is likely a wide margin of error.

Our asset index results are as expected: respondents with a higher score on the asset index are also happier (see Table 3.6).[24] We also find that

[24] Respondents that received a socio-economic assessment from the interviewers were also happier than the average, although when we include this assessment and our asset index in the same regression, the latter becomes insignificant. It is likely that the interviewers' assessments were based on asset ownership.

Table 3.6 Happiness in Afghanistan

Explanatory variables	Description of variables	Dependent variable: happy					
		Reg 1		Reg 2		Reg 3	
age	in years	−0.0140	(0.001)**	−0.0040	(0.000)**	−0.0050	−0.205
age²	Age squared	0.0000	(0.033)*	0.0000	−0.410	0.0000	−0.343
married	Dummy: 1=married 0=others	−0.0030	−0.955	−0.0050	−0.933	0.0090	−0.868
gender	Dummy: 1=male 0=female	0.0310	−0.437	0.0980	−0.173	0.0920	−0.199
unemp	Dummy: 1=unemployed	−0.1440	(0.042)*	−0.0910	−0.189	−0.1060	−0.125
hhinc1	Household asset index	0.6360	(0.000)**	0.0190	−0.870	0.0140	−0.899
tlbn	Dummy: 1=strong Taliban influence in province 0=other	0.2470	(0.000)**	0.1680	(0.001)**	0.1760	(0.001)**
headhh	Dummy: respondent head of HH			−0.1160	(0.023)*	−0.1080	(0.034)*
lls	Position of life on a 10-point scale			0.0410	(0.000)**	0.0470	(0.000)**
els	Economic condition on a 10-point scale			0.0390	(0.006)**	0.0290	(0.037)*
outlook	Perception of economic outlook			0.4850	(0.000)**	0.4810	(0.000)**
frchoice	Freedom of choice			0.0250	(0.002)**	0.0250	(0.002)**
frexpr	Freedom of expression			0.0350	(0.047)*	0.0370	(0.032)*
satdemo	Satisfaction with democracy			0.1020	(0.000)**	0.1030	(0.000)**
vcrime	Dummy: crime victim in the last 12 months					−0.0350	−0.590
vcorr	Dummy: corruption victim in the last 12 months			−0.0730	−0.120		
Constant		2.6830	(0.000)**	1.1640	(0.000)**	1.1870	(0.000)**
Observations		1936		1717		1727	
R²		0.052		0.201		0.197	

Notes: p values in parentheses below the coefficients.
* significant at 5%; ** significant at 1%.

respondents with higher levels of self-assessed economic status—via the ladder question—are happier than the average, as are respondents with a positive economic outlook for the future. It is quite likely some of this is driven by perceptions being auto-correlated as much as it is by real economic differences: happier people are more likely to be optimistic about the economic future, as well as to place themselves higher on the economic ladder. The role of perceptions may be particularly important in the Afghan context, where normal measures of economic activity and progress, such as reported income, have less significance due to the extra legal or informal nature of much economic activity. Indeed, when we include our perceived economic indicators in the same regression as the asset index, the latter becomes insignificant, suggesting that the correlation between perceived economic status and happiness is much stronger than that between objective economic indicators and happiness.

Our findings on political freedom are notable, meanwhile. Those respondents that are satisfied with democracy as a system of government are also happier than others, although we cannot establish a direction of causality. Those respondents that believe that they can speak out freely, without repression, are significantly happier than others, suggesting that freedom does matter to well-being, even in a context where it is rare or under threat as in Afghanistan. Indeed, one could argue that it matters more precisely because it is under threat, which is the opposite of an adaptation story.

Respondents who live in Taliban-influenced areas are, on average, happier than the average. It is very important to note that these are *not* Taliban-controlled areas, but rather those where there is more open presence of the Taliban. The two provinces that we interviewed are in the south, and indeed are the only southern provinces in the sample that are in our data set. There are some things about the south—such as more religiosity in general—which could affect our findings and we indeed find that our respondents from these two regions report being more devout than the average. There may also be some unobservable things about the regions where we interviewed that could strongly influence happiness, but they are difficult to measure and likely have nothing to do with the Taliban.

The respondents in these two provinces were overwhelmingly male (which is not a surprise). They were also, rather surprisingly, more likely to be satisfied with democracy and more likely to say that they had freedom of expression, but less likely to say that they had freedom of choice to do what they wanted with their lives. Rather surprisingly, and in contrast with most other contexts, respondents who had been a victim of either crime or corruption in the last 12 months were no less happy than the average in Afghanistan. As crime and corruption have become the norm, there seems to have been a significant amount of adaptation which has mediated the usual effects of these phenomena on well-being. Supporting this interpretation, other variables that proxy safety and freedom from crime, such as being able to walk safely in your neighborhood, also had no significant effects on happiness. This is a very marked departure from most other places in the world, where being a crime or corruption victim is clearly negative for happiness, and being able to walk safely is positive for happiness. The findings run in the same direction, though, as some of our findings in Latin America on adaptation to crime and corruption in environments where high levels of these phenomena are the norm, and where adaptation also mediates their well-being effects. These are discussed in detail in Chapter 7.

In contrast, though, respondents in the Taliban-influenced areas who reported that they had been victims of corruption were significantly less happy than the average, suggesting that there is less tolerance for and/or adaptation to corruption in those areas. Supporting such an interpretation, respondents in these areas were also less tolerant of tax evasion than the average (as gauged by a question that asked respondents how acceptable it was to evade taxes in their country). (Regression results available from the author.)

Perhaps what is most notable about our findings is the extent to which there is consistency across the most basic variables (age, income, perceived economic status, and so on) even in the tumultuous economic and political context that the Afghan people are living in. We also find evidence of adaptation to high levels of crime and corruption. Equally important is the extent to which the relationships between happiness and freedom, and happiness and democracy, hold in such a context. It may be that people are more adaptable to certain phenomena, such as crime and corruption, than they are in the case of more fundamental public goods, such as freedom and democratic government, particularly if the latter are under threat.

Conclusions

In exploring happiness in a number of contexts around the world, we find a remarkable amount of consistency in the socio-economic and demographic determinants of happiness. The *modest* differences that we find across countries and regions are usually explained by *major* differences in economic contexts or education and labor market structures. In this sense, happiness surveys not only tell us about variance in happiness across the contexts, but shed light on what the contextual factors are.

Studies by psychologists find that most individuals have fairly stable levels of happiness or subjective well-being, but that those levels are also subject to short-term fluctuations. Our look at happiness around the world supports the idea that there are different elements of well-being, some of which are behaviorally driven and others determined by socio-economic and demographic variables. The latter are much more vulnerable to day-to-day events, such as changes in employment and marital status, as well as fluctuations in income. These in turn differ across country contexts and tend to be more variable in the developing and transition economies than they are in developed ones. Regardless, the basic determinants of happiness across these country contexts—and across widely different levels of per capita incomes—are remarkably similar, perhaps because of the strong role for psychological traits in determining happiness levels.

Our most comparable and robust results are the comparisons between Latin America and Russia, on the one hand, and the United States and Europe on the other. Here we find a remarkable amount of consistency in the determinants of happiness across very different regional contexts. To the extent that there are differences, they seem to reflect the nature of employment and safety net structures (the unhappy self-employed in Latin America and the unhappy pensioners in Russia); minority and gender rights (happy minorities in Russia as opposed to unhappy minorities in the United States and Latin America; less happiness among women in Latin America than in the United States; unhappy marriages in Russia). Otherwise, there are strong similarities in how age, income, education, health, and unemployment, as well as attitudes about upward mobility, correlate with happiness across these regions.

We also got a bird's-eye view into some other regions. Our Central Asia findings demonstrated similarities with those for the rest of the world, with some modest differences in the role of trust and other social capital variables. This perhaps reflects the extent to which these recently independent countries are still forging a social contract and that political freedom is incomplete. Our findings for Cuba, meanwhile, while not directly comparable to the other happiness surveys, did suggest that the absence of economic freedom in that country was linked to lower levels of well-being, at least according to some measures. In contrast, Easterlin's (2008) work on Eastern Europe, where a major transition to economic freedom occurred at the expense of widely available social safety nets, finds that satisfaction with the material situation has increased as a result, but that the general life satisfaction of vulnerable groups has fallen at the same time.

Our findings for Africa, meanwhile, are the least comparable, but perhaps the most provocative. Given the incomplete nature of the data and that the questions that we used are merely proxies, our findings must be taken with a grain of salt. To the extent that they do accurately reflect realities, though, they suggest that attitudes in Africa depart from those found elsewhere in the world, reflecting higher levels of optimism about the future among the poor than for other groups, while in the rest of the world, higher levels of optimism are correlated with higher levels of income. We are not sure whether optimism per se (that which is not explained by objective circumstances) plays a role in helping the poorest survive in Africa, or whether it merely reflects the ability of individuals to adjust their own expectations downward in adverse circumstances while maintaining hope for better lives for their children.

Similar to Africa, Afghanistan is another context where individuals have to cope with extreme adversity and seem to be able to either maintain natural cheerfulness or to adapt their expectations downwards. Mean happiness levels in Afghanistan were only slightly lower than those for Latin America, for example. At the same time, respondents in Afghanistan were realistic— or at least relatively more pessimistic than their happiness levels suggest— when they assessed their own lives compared to the best possible life. Mean responses on this question for Afghanistan were significantly below those for Latin America and for the world average as well. At the individual level, what is most notable about our findings is the extent to which there is consistency across the most basic variables (age, income, perceived economic status, and so on) even in the tumultuous economic and political context that the Afghan people are living in. Equally important is the extent to which the relationships between happiness and freedom, and happiness and democracy, hold in such a context.

At this point in the look at happiness around the world, a point at which we have discovered remarkable consistency in the basic determinants of happiness across countries in very different contexts, an obvious question is: does happiness matter? Do happier people live better lives? Do they work harder or enjoy their lives more? Are they healthier? Until now we have explored the question of what matters to happiness. In the next chapter, we ask if happiness matters in relation to other things that we care about, such as better health and performance in the labor market.

CHAPTER 4

Does Happiness Matter?[1]

The last few chapters were spent trying to understand what makes people happy and how that varies across countries, cultures, and levels of development. We care about happiness for all sorts of reasons. Some are philosophical: the pursuit of happiness has consumed our conceptual and theoretical interest for centuries. Some are psychological: we worry about those who are deeply unhappy and debilitated by it and, at the same time, we are inspired by those who are very happy despite seemingly insurmountable odds. But, at a more concrete level, does happiness matter from the perspective of the variables that policymakers care about and are able to influence? Do happier people perform better in the labor market? Do they save and invest more in their children's future? Are happier people healthier? Does happiness matter to future outcomes?

In both Latin America and Russia, we find that happier people are more likely to support market policies, to be satisfied with how democracy was working, and to prefer democracy to any other system of government

[1] This section of the chapter draws heavily from Graham et al. (2004).

(see Chapter 6). Happier people, on average, have higher prospects for their own and their children's future mobility (POUM); are more likely to believe that the distribution of income in their country was fair; place themselves higher on a notional economic ladder; and have lower fear of unemployment.[2] The POUM question asks respondents about their own and their children's future situation compared to today's. The economic ladder question (ELQ) asks respondents to place themselves on a ten-step ladder representing their society, where the poor are on step one and the rich are on step ten. Support for market policies was measured by an index based on several scaled questions about the private sector, foreign investment, free trade, and privatization. What we do not know, for the most part, though, is what the direction of causality is. It may be that happier people are more likely to be satisfied with whatever policy framework they live in and are just naturally more optimistic. But does happiness—or natural optimism—have causal effects on future behaviors and outcomes?

For example, are married people happier, or are happier people more likely to get married? Are wealthier people happier, or are happier people more likely to be successful and earn more income over time? Similar questions can be posed in a number of areas, including the positive relationship between health and happiness, between happiness and support for market policies and democracy, and happiness and tolerance for inequality.

One of the primary difficulties in establishing this direction of causality is the lack of adequate data. Most of the happiness research is based on cross-section data (one-time interviews of a large cross-section of a population or various populations), while to answer these questions, we need panel data (i.e. surveys that follow the same people over time. Such

---

[2] For detail, see Graham and Pettinato (2002a).

data are particularly rare for developing countries). A few isolated studies by psychologists in the United States and Australia indicate that happier people earn more income in later periods than do their less happy cohorts, yet for the most part, research on subjective well-being has not addressed these questions.[3]

Using the Russian panel data from the Russian Longitudinal Monitoring Survey (RLMS), Andrew Eggers, Sandip Sukhtankar, and I examined happiness data on the same individuals for two points in time and examine a number of questions in which the direction of causality is not clear from cross-section data alone.[4] Our central goal was to test whether people who reported higher happiness in 1995 than would be expected, based on their socio-economic and demographic characteristics, to have fared differently in 2000 than others. Presumably, these differences are due to psychological or other non-economic or demographic factors. The purpose was to determine whether these differences, appearing in people's reported happiness levels in the first period, have effects on outcomes such as income, marriage status, and employment in the second.

Psychologists find that there is a remarkable degree of consistency in people's level of well-being over time. They attribute this stability in happiness levels to homeostasis, in which happiness levels are not only under the influence of experience, but also controlled by positive cognitive

[3] These effects seem to be more important for those at the higher end of the income ladder. Diener and Biswas-Diener (2008).

[4] The 2000 results were not available at the time of that analysis. See Graham and Pettinato (2002b). In addition, the *Journal of Happiness Studies* had a special issue on happiness in Russia (2(2) 2001) that was based on the analysis of a separate panel of households, the Russet panel, which ran from 1993 to 1995. The articles in that volume tracked changes in happiness over time, but did not attempt to evaluate the effects of happiness on other variables such as income. See, for example, Veenhoven (2002).

bias such as self-esteem, control, and optimism.[5] Our objective in this research was to see whether this psychological component of happiness made any difference to people's performance in the labor market and in the health arena, and potentially in other areas where individual effort and performance matters to their later well-being.

The RLMS data for Russia is rare in that it is a large panel, covering an average of almost 13,000 Russians per year from 1992 to 2001 and from which we created a panel data set containing data in 1995 and 2000.[6] One drawback of the data set, however, is that it covers a time period in Russia when there was a tremendous amount of economic and structural change that affected many people's livelihood and economic well-being. This is a context which is much more typical of economies in transition or developing economies, than of more established market economies. Thus there were likely more than usual fluctuations in happiness levels that pertained to the very difficult economic and social conditions people had to live through. Yet this same instability in economic conditions provides us with a better than average reference point for assessing stability in subjective well-being or happiness levels that is independent of changes in economic conditions. In other words, to the extent that we can identify character traits that are specific to particular individuals and hold over time, we can be fairly sure that they are robust to major structural changes in the context respondents are living in.

[5] See, for example, Cummins and Nistico (2002).

[6] The RLMS is a nationally representative panel study for Russia, carried out in collaboration with the University of North Carolina at Chapel Hill and with funding from USAID among others. More information on the survey can be found at http://www.cpc.unc.edu/projects/rlms/. Critics of the survey question its degree of representativeness. Accepting that some of these criticisms may have validity, we nevertheless believe it is an extremely valuable data set.

Russia in the 1990s

Any attempts to generalize from analysis based on Russia in the 1990s must take into account the far-reaching nature of the changes in that country's economy and polity over the course of the decade. During that period, Russia underwent a transition from a centrally planned economy and communist government to a free market, presidential-parliamentary democracy.[7] At the same time, much of its large federation—which was part and parcel of its status as a superpower—was parceled into a number of newly independent states.

The transition had high social costs, with some of the worst losers being pensioners and others on fixed incomes. Poverty and inequality increased markedly. Depending on the data sources, the prevalence of poverty in Russia was between 22 and 33% in 2001, while the Gini coefficient increased from 0.29 to 0.40 between 1992 and 1998, with some estimates as high as 0.48, a level which is comparable to some of the most unequal countries in Latin America.[8] An additional shock, particularly to those on fixed incomes, came from a financial crisis and sharp devaluation of the ruble in August 1998. The devaluation, in which the ruble fell to 25% of its previous rate against the US dollar, was accompanied by fiscal austerity.[9]

Since the crisis and devaluation, Russia's economy has experienced positive growth rates for several years in a row. Yet a large part of Russia's economy remains 'virtual'—outside the monetary, market economy.

[7] This is Freedom House's classification of the government in Russia in 2002.

[8] There is considerable debate over these figures, in part due to problems with accurate data over time. These figures are from the World Bank (http:// www.worldbank.org.ru). For a more detailed discussion, see, for example, Klugman and Braithwaite (1998); Van Praag and Ferrer-i-Carbonell (2004).

[9] See Gaddy and Ickes (2002).

Numerous city-sized factories throughout Russia conduct a large share of their transactions on a non-monetary basis. Their workers in turn receive their wages and benefits in kind. To survive, Russians engage in extensive self-subsistence activity, beginning with food production. Russians—and this includes not only rural residents but also middle-class urban professionals, such as scientists, doctors, and military officers—produce an astounding 50% of the nation's meat supply and 80% of all vegetables and fruits on their family garden plots.[10] Russia's 'virtual' economy acts as a de facto safety net, limiting the impact of devaluation-induced price changes on the average consumer at the time of devaluation, for example.

There is considerable debate over the extent to which Russia's transition to the market has been a success or a failure, and whether the pace and sequencing of reform was appropriate. This is a debate that is well beyond the scope of this chapter.[11] Yet it is important to recognize that our panel data cover a period of extensive economic and political change, and the effects of those changes have not been even across individuals and across economic sectors. This, in turn, could affect the relationship between income and well-being.

There are some peculiarities in the data that seem to reflect the reality of the Russian situation—in terms of both a large black market and a large barter or virtual economy.[12] For example, we had 54 observations from respondents who reported zero household income. Yet the results of our econometric analysis including these respondents produced results which were quite counter-intuitive, such as a consistently positive and significant sign on the zero income dummies in relation to both future happiness and

[10] For detail on this, see Gaddy and Ickes (2002).
[11] For a critical view, see Stiglitz (2002). For a more optimistic view, see Aslund (1995).
[12] For a description of Russia's 'virtual economy', see Gaddy and Ickes (2002).

future income. About half of the zero income respondents reported that they were employed. It is quite plausible that they are earning substantial income on the black market, which they are reluctant to report, and/or have earnings in kind. These earnings still have effects on their well-being, but do not show up as reported income.[13]

Another caveat is that all panel data suffer from attrition bias. Those on the extreme tails of the distribution are the most likely to drop out of the panel, as the wealthiest may move to better neighborhoods and the poorest who 'don't make it' may move in with other family members or opt for other kinds of coping strategies. Thus panels can be biased in their representation of all income groups. In the case of Russia, with extreme levels of economic and political turmoil, it is plausible that this attrition occurs more than it would under more stable circumstances. Our analysis of the data, however, finds no difference between the characteristics of those respondents in the panel and the entire group of respondents in the original 1995 survey, at least as measured by age, education, income, gender, marital status, and happiness.[14]

[13] We initially attempted to include these respondents by adding one to each of the 54 observations that reported zero household income in order to take a log and include them. We also created a dummy variable for these respondents, in order to control for any effects that were specific to them and/or that resulted from our arbitrary specification of their income level (adding one). We also substituted this specification with a Box-Cox income variable transformation, but found that it did not have a (statistically significant) better fit than did the zero-plus-one logarithmic specification with zero income dummies. Including them produces skewed results (e.g. log income in 1995 was negatively correlated with log income in 2000). Since they comprise only 54 observations in a sample of over 5,000, we chose to drop them and to use a simple log equivalence specification throughout the analysis. Results of this econometric analysis are available from the authors on request.

[14] Results available from the authors on request.

A second problem, measurement error, involves possible error stemming from the difficulty of accurately measuring the incomes of those individuals who work in the informal economy or in the agricultural sector. As noted above, this informal sector is disproportionately large in Russia.[15]

There are also concerns that, because of Russia's political legacy, respondents might view survey questions with suspicion and answer them less honestly then they would in other contexts. Thus, the unusually low levels of happiness in Russia could be due to such suspicions, or to unfavorable comparisons with the West, and/or to a culture of negativism. However, research by Veenhoven (2002) finds that the unusually low levels of happiness in Russia have more to do with the troublesome transitions than with Russian national character or other biases in responses. Finally, despite these many caveats, the relatively large sample size and the intuitive nature of many of our results make us cautiously optimistic about their broader applicability.

Changes in Happiness in Russia, 1995–2000

Happiness research finds general patterns in the relationship between socio-economic variables and happiness across countries and across time, but with subtle variations. Given the extent of economic change and mobility in Russia during the period under study, we expected there to be more than the usual variation across time. The 1990s crisis hit retirees, the

---

[15] We attempted to deal with this error in our sample by creating dummy variables for the 54 respondents that reported zero income. Rather ironically, at least half of these respondents display other traits that suggest they have substantial assets if not monetary income (discussed below). Because of this, including them often skewed our econometric results and thus we did not include them in most of our analysis.

Table 4.1 The correlates of happiness, Russia, 1995 and 2000
Dependent variable: happiness (ordered logit regression).

Independent variables	1995		2000		t-stat for Equivalence
	Coef.	z	Coef.	z	
Age	−0.0742	−6.27	−0.0668	−7.42	0.498
Age^2	0.0008	6.35	0.0007	7.15	−0.498
Male	0.1419	2.41	0.1521	2.80	0.128
Married	0.1490	2.15	0.0875	1.40	−0.659
Log equivalence income	**0.4777**	13.97	**0.3892**	11.48	**−1.839**
Education level	0.0305	1.87	0.0150	0.96	−0.688
Minority	**0.3835**	5.21	**0.1721**	2.46	**−2.082**
Student	0.4561	2.91	0.1991	1.59	−1.281
Retired	−0.3029	−3.05	−0.3783	−3.97	−0.548
Housewife	0.1814	1.34	0.0490	0.33	−0.661
Unemployed	**−0.2434**	−2.19	**−0.6568**	−6.51	**−2.756**
Self-employed	0.7676	3.00	0.5375	2.23	−0.654
Health index	0.2744	2.22	0.4462	3.82	1.010
Observations	4524		5134		
Pseudo R^2	0.0330		0.0331		

unemployed, and lenders particular very hard. Rather remarkably, there was very little change in the relationship among the standard variables and happiness during this time period. When we tested the difference between the two-years' results, however, the only two coefficients that experienced a significant change in value were being a minority and being unemployed; even then there was no change in direction in the sign of either coefficient, see Table 4.1.

In 2000, while minorities were still, on average, happier than other respondents, they were far less happy than they were in 1995. The war in Chechnya, which started at about the time the first survey was conducted, has changed the image of Muslims and minorities in general in Russia, and a number of surveys find that the majority of Russians support the efforts of their military against a mainly Islamic population.[16] Thus respondents who are Muslim or minorities have, on average, higher happiness levels than Russians, but have experienced a transitory (one hopes) decline in happiness due to the change in the status of Muslims related to the war.

The second coefficient that experienced a change in value was being unemployed. While unemployed people were less happy on average than others in both years, the negative effects of being unemployed were significantly greater in 2000 than they were in 1995. This probably reflects the effects of the financial crisis and the devaluation on the fixed and/or very meager incomes of the unemployed.

If our simple cross-sectional model completely captured the determinants of happiness, then conducting a panel fixed effects regression—essentially, measuring the effect of *changes* in the determinants on *changes* in happiness, while holding constant the traits that are unique to each individual respondent—would produce identical coefficient results. However, we have good reason to believe that the fixed effects regression will yield different and better estimates.

Most importantly, panel fixed effects analysis corrects some of the bias associated with unobserved characteristics of the survey respondents in cross-sectional analysis, by holding constant the information that we have available for each individual respondent and examining the changes in other variables. Although we observe a great many characteristics of each respondent, these factors leave much of the variation in happiness unexplained (the R-squared—e.g. explanatory power—in our happiness

---

[16] See Gerber and Mendelson (2002).

models is in the neighborhood of 0.03, suggesting that about 97% of the variation in happiness responses is due to factors we do not observe). For example, a person's disposition or personality is assuredly one of the determinants of their level of reported happiness, so we would expect a person with a generally sunnier disposition to report a higher level of happiness than a person who is identical in every other respect but has a gloomier outlook. Disposition, of course, is not captured in survey data.

These unobserved determinants of happiness can bias our coefficient estimates in cross-sectional analysis. For example, if a person's disposition affects both his income and his happiness results in the same way, then our estimate of the effect of income on happiness will be biased upwards, since disposition is unobserved. Using panel data allows us to filter out the set of unobserved determinants of happiness that are unchanging over time, which should remove this bias and improve upon our coefficient estimates from cross-sectional analysis.

One potential problem with conducting panel fixed effects analysis with this data set comes from the volatility of Russian society in the period for which we have data. The relationship between observed characteristics and happiness changed between 1995 and 2000, which we believe reflects an adjustment of Russians' priorities and concerns in the course of dramatic social change. Accordingly, some of the respondents' change in happiness that we analyze in this exercise will be attributable to this change in priorities rather than to a change in their observable circumstances.

On the other hand, the volatility in late-1990s Russia can be seen as a unique opportunity for analysis. Panel studies rely on changes in the observed variables to detect causal effects, so panel studies on populations that change very little tend to be unrevealing. Yet in this instance, most likely due to the extensive economic changes in Russia during the period, the data reveal a high degree of mobility. There was significantly more movement among income quintiles in the second half of the 1990s (1995–2000) in Russia than there was during the entire 1980s in the United States, for example. Happiness levels also fluctuated a great deal during the period, with downward shifts more common than upward ones.

The results of our fixed effects analysis are reported in Table 4.2. We find that the only variables that have significant effects on changes in happiness are changes in income, which has positive effects; getting divorced, which has negative effects; and leaving school, which also has negative effects. The effects of income and divorce are both unsurprising, and would probably hold in any context. The effects of leaving school, which may or may not hold in other contexts, are intuitive in the Russian context, where the labor market is very precarious, and highly educated people are often unable to find satisfactory jobs.

Finally, it is quite interesting that while both unemployment and retirement are negatively correlated with happiness in our standard regression, neither retiring nor becoming unemployed had significant effects in the panel regression. This may reflect the rather mixed fate of pensioners and the unemployed in Russia. Recent retirees are probably much better prepared to cope with the current economic environment than are those who retired many years ago on fixed incomes.[17] And many jobs in Russia pay unstable, if any, wages, while many highly educated workers are often overqualified for what they are doing, which may mitigate the usual effects of becoming unemployed on happiness.

[17] This contrasts with findings for the United States, for example, where workers are least happy in anticipation of retirement, but then happier, on average, after they retire. See the chapter by Lowenstein et al. in Aaron (1999).

Table 4.2 First difference regression—happiness in Russia

Dependent variable: change in happiness, 1995 to 2000 (ordered logit regression).

	Coef.	z
Static variables		
age	−0.0400	−1.70
age^2	0.0004	1.54
male	0.0390	0.35
minority	−0.0632	−0.51
Changes in continuous variables		
change in log equivalence income	**0.1875**	**4.21**
change in education level	0.0312	0.62
change in health index	0.0757	0.47
change in level of drinking	−0.0102	−0.31
Changes in status variables:		
Marriage (omitted group: remained single)		
got married	−0.3802	−1.20
got divorced	**−0.5681**	**−3.20**
stayed married	−0.1905	−1.57
Employment (omitted: remained unemployed)		
got employed	0.0608	0.19
got unemployed	−0.2054	−0.65
stayed employed	0.3554	1.35
Smoking (omitted: remained a non-smoker)		
quit smoking	0.1451	0.58
started smoking	0.2488	1.19
kept smoking	−0.0356	−0.31
Schooling (omitted: remained a non-student)		
entered school	*	*
left school	**−0.8415**	**−2.38**
stayed in school	−0.7139	−1.29
Retirement (omitted: remained a non-retiree)		
became retired	−0.0699	−0.38
came out of retirement	0.2638	0.55
stayed retired	−0.0731	−0.35
Observations	1673	
Pseudo R^2	0.0089	

Notes: *Dropped because of multi-colinearity.

Does Happiness Matter to Future Outcomes?

Having established the basic patterns in happiness in Russia (reported in Chapter 3), and then changes in those patterns from 1995 to 2000 (reported above), we took advantage of our over time data to see if the happiness that we measured in our first period of observation had any effects on various outcomes in the second period. We used our panel data to create a 'residual' or unexplained happiness variable, which was an attempt to capture or proxy this psychological element of happiness. This was achieved through a simple two-stage regression process. In the first stage, we explored the primary determinants of happiness in the first year for which we had data. As we have done in so many other instances in our study of happiness, we explored how important differences were among the standard variables, such as age, gender, marital and employment status, and income, to happiness in our sample of respondents. As is reported in Chapter 3, the determinants of happiness in Russia are quite similar to those for the United States and Latin America, with slight differences: men are happier than women, retired people are significantly less happy, and married people are no happier than the average.

In the next stage, we used the residual from the first-stage regressions—in other words, the happiness that was not explained by the standard socio-demographic variables analyzed above—to create an 'unexplained' or residual happiness variable for each respondent. This unexplained happiness variable captures psychological differences among respondents in our sample (as well as some noise). We then used this unexplained happiness variable as an independent variable in regressions with second stage income and second stage health as dependent variables. In layman's terms, we asked whether this unexplained happiness for each respondent mattered to their outcomes in later years. Simply put: does happiness pay? Does happiness make you healthier? Does happiness make you more likely to get married or get divorced?

We found that happier people earn more income in later periods, on average, than less happy people. This was based on our second stage regressions, in which we included our residual as an independent variable with second period income as the dependent variable. Controlling for first period income, we found that our residual had positive and significant effects on second period income, see Table 4.3.

Accepting that there is a large margin for error and/or correlated error in this analysis, our results suggest that happier people seem to earn more income and/or perform better in the labor market. Psychologists attribute traits, such as positive outlook and high self-esteem (so-called positive cognitive bias), to happier people. It is not surprising that these traits also contribute to productivity.

We also found that the correlation between happiness and future income was stronger for those at lower levels of income, while the role of first period income was more important for future income for those at higher levels of income. A positive outlook and high self-esteem may be valuable labor market assets for those with fewer assets or income, particularly for those who provide services. These traits probably matter less for those who have sufficient income or assets to leverage in making future gains.

We also looked at a number of attitudinal variables. As discussed in other chapters, attitudes about future mobility (prospects of upward mobility or POUM) for oneself and for one's children are linked to higher happiness levels, to lower discount rates (e.g. willingness to trade-off present consumption for future benefit), and to lower support for

Table 4.3 The effects of happiness on income in Russia, 1995–2000
Dependent variable: log equivalence income, 2000 (OLS).

Independent variables	a Coef.	a t	b Coef.	b t	c Coef.	c t
Age	−0.013	−3.00	−0.013	−2.97	−0.015	−3.25
Age^2	0.000	3.18	0.000	3.15	0.000	3.52
Male	0.010	0.42	0.010	0.42	0.000	−0.02
Married	0.205	7.84	0.205	7.84	0.205	7.84
Education level	0.030	4.51	0.030	4.51	0.030	4.44
Minority	0.121	3.98	0.123	4.03	0.122	4.00
Student	−0.034	−0.34	−0.030	−0.31	−0.037	−0.38
Retired	−0.191	−4.85	−0.190	−4.83	−0.166	−4.18
Housewife	−0.249	−3.90	−0.249	−3.90	−0.239	−3.73
Unemployed	−0.345	−8.16	−0.344	−8.12	−0.343	−8.07
Self-employed	0.142	1.46	0.141	1.46	0.128	1.33
Health index	0.060	1.11	0.059	1.09	0.056	1.04
Log equiv income 95	0.242	18.11	0.243	18.12	0.224	15.69
Log equiv income 95, poor**	*	*	*	*	0.009	2.60
Log equiv income 95, rich**	*	*	*	*	0.018	4.36
Unexplained happiness, 95***	**0.030**	**2.64**	**0.063**	**2.32**	**0.027**	**2.38**
Unexp. happiness, 95***, 2nd quint.	*	*	−0.044	−1.14	*	*
Unexp. happiness, 95***, 3rd quint.	*	*	−0.036	−0.95	*	*
Unexp. happiness, 95***, 4th quint.	*	*	−0.063	−1.71	*	*
Unexp. happiness, 95***, 5th quint.	*	*	−0.023	−0.65	*	*
constant	5.833	36.35	5.823	36.19	5.936	34.62
Number of observations	4457		4457		4457	
Adjusted R^2	*0.134*		*0.133*		*0.152*	

Notes: * omitted.
** 'poor' is defined as bottom 40% of the income distribution in 1995; 'rich' is the top 20%.
*** the residual of basic happiness 1995 regression.
Regression a: no income quintile distinctions.
Regression b: testing for a difference in the effect of unexplained happiness on 2000 income, by 1995 income quintile.
Regression c: testing for a difference in the effect of 1995 income on 2000 income, by 1995 income quintile.
Independent variables are from 2000 unless otherwise noted.

Source: Graham et al. (2004).

redistribution (at least in the United States). We calculated our unexplained perceptions variables in the same way that we calculated our unexplained happiness variable. In a first stage, we ran the same regressions as in the case of happiness, but with each perceptions variable (POUM, ELQ, and fear of unemployment) as the dependent variable, and the usual socio-demographic variables as controls. Our 'unexplained' POUM, ELQ, and fear of unemployment were then, in turn, the variance in these attitudes across people that is not explained by contextual and demographic factors. Perhaps a simpler way to explain this is that in a comparison between two people of the same age, gender, income level, education, employment status, and so on, who have very different outlooks for the future, our unexplained perceptions variable would account for or pick up that difference between them. We found that these perceptions variables had a similar relationship with future income as did our unexplained happiness variable.

Having a high POUM or placing oneself high on the notional economic ladder (ELQ) in the first period was positively correlated with higher levels of income in the second period. In contrast, having higher fear of unemployment was negatively correlated with future income (albeit only significant at the 10% level), see Table 4.4.

Respondents' views or attitudes about their future prospects are correlated with their future outcomes and may play a role in determining those outcomes. It is likely that both happiness and perceptions variables are picking up similar character traits, such as optimism and self-esteem.[18] Whatever the combination of character traits these variables are picking up, they seem to be linked to better outcomes in the income earnings arena. While this is somewhat intuitive, and supported by the work of some

---

[18] It is, of course, possible that these results are error driven as well.

Table 4.4 Effect of perceptions variables on future income in Russia, 1995–2000
Dependent variable: log equivalence income in 2000 (OLS).

Independent variables	a		b	
	Coef.	t	Coef.	t
Age	−0.013	−3.00	−0.009	−0.78
Age^2	0.000	3.18	0.000	1.24
Male	0.010	0.42	−0.008	−0.23
Married	0.205	7.84	0.241	6.15
Education level	0.030	4.51	0.032	2.44
Minority	0.121	3.98	0.081	1.80
Student	−0.034	−0.34	0.427	1.07
Retired	−0.191	−4.85	−0.273	−4.60
Housewife	−0.249	−3.90	−0.166	−1.60
Unemployed	−0.345	−8.16	−0.373	−5.82
Self-employed	0.142	1.46	0.094	0.72
Health index	0.060	1.11	0.061	0.84
Log equiv income 96	0.242	18.11	0.230	11.55
Unexplained happiness, 95**	**0.030**	**2.64**	**−0.002**	**−0.11**
Fear of unemployment, 95	*	*	−0.014	−1.22
Family better off next year, 95	*	*	0.041	2.27
Economic ladder question, 95	*	*	0.027	2.17
Constant	5.833	36.35	5.533	17.49
Observations	4457		2296	
Adjusted R^2	*0.134*		*0.126*	

Notes: * omitted.
** the residual of basic happiness in 1995 regression.
Independent variables are from 2000 unless otherwise noted.
Regression a: no perceptions variables.
Regression b: perceptions variables included.

Source: Graham et al. (2004).

psychologists, such as Diener and Biswas-Diener (2008), it has rarely—
if ever—been documented in a large-scale sample of respondents using
econometric techniques.

A caveat, of course, is that it is plausible that some of what we find is
explained by people's abilities to forecast or predict their future income, and

thus first period attitudes merely reflect people's knowledge of the future. The highly unstable nature of the Russian context, however, renders this unlikely as the *entire* explanation. There is broader psychological evidence that character traits have effects on individuals' labor market performance and on their health outcomes.[19] It may be that behavioral or attitudinal variables may be more important in extremely uncertain contexts, such as Russia, where it is more difficult to predict the future. Research based on comparable data for other countries is necessary to test such a proposition.

Marriage, Employment, Health, and Smoking and Drinking

One of our most important findings is that unexplained or residual happiness has positive effects on future income. An additional question, which we explore in this section, is if unexplained happiness also has effects on other socio-economic variables, such as on the probability of getting married or divorced, of being healthy, of being unemployed, and on behaviors such as smoking and drinking.

As expected, married people are, on average, happier than non-married people in Russia in 2000.[20] We created dummy variables for changes in marital status during the 1995–2000 period. Forty-five percent of the

[19] Cummins and Nistico (2002); Diener and Seligman (2004).

[20] One interesting finding is that, in 1995, married people were not significantly happier than others, a finding that supports our intuition that overall happiness levels increased from 1995 to 2000. (For happiness in 1995, see Graham and Pettinato, 2002b.) This is supported by the fact that 35% of the sample had positive changes in happiness levels, while 28% had decreases, plus the general improvements on the economic and governance fronts in Russia during the period.

sample—2,935 respondents—stayed married, while others experienced a change in status: 226 respondents (or 3% of the sample) got married and 529 respondents (or 8% of the sample) got divorced. Our first set of regressions explored whether residual or unexplained happiness was a predictor of change in marital status. Rather surprisingly, given the strong relationship between marriage and happiness, there was no significant relationship between residual happiness and getting married. In other words, happier people are not more likely than others to get married. (See Table 4.2.)

Divorce is a marital status variable that has notable effects on happiness in most studies: divorced individuals are, on average, less happy than others. This is also the case in our Russia data set. Becoming divorced had negative and significant effects on both happiness levels in 2000 and changes in happiness levels from 1995 to 2000 in Russia. Yet we found that residual happiness—or, more accurately put, unhappiness—had no significant effect on the probability of getting divorced.[21] (Table 4.5) Thus while unhappiness does not cause divorce, divorce clearly causes unhappiness. In contrast, when we looked at the effects of getting married on happiness and changes in happiness, the sign on the coefficient was positive, but it was (rather surprisingly) insignificant for both variables (see Table 4.3).

Not surprisingly, given the consistently negative effects of unemployment on happiness across countries and time, those who became unemployed in our sample were significantly less happy than other respondents. Unexplained happiness, however, had no significant effects on the probability of being employed (the sign on the coefficient is negative but not significant).

---

[21] The reverse of this was also true: residual happiness had no significant effects on the probability of staying married.

Table 4.5 The effects of happiness on marriage status, employment, and health

Dependent variable: Condition: Regression technique: Independent variables	Divorce by 2000 (given married 1995) Logit a Coef.	z	Married by 2000 (given unmarried 1995) Logit b Coef.	z	Unemployed in 2000 Logit c Coef.	z	2000 health index OLS d Coef.	t
Age	−0.1061	−4.00	0.1023	2.12	0.1609	3.86	−0.0023	−1.89
Age^2	0.0012	4.57	−0.0017	−2.71	−0.0023	−4.62	0.0000	0.97
Male	−0.8974	−7.50	0.1331	0.62	0.8566	6.85	0.0319	4.76
Married	*		*		−0.3410	−2.55	0.0109	1.51
Education level	−0.0134	−0.43	−0.0171	−0.21	0.0356	0.71	−0.0001	−0.04
Minority	−0.2832	−1.77	−0.1190	−0.44	0.4020	2.94	0.0129	1.54
Student	**		−1.1540	−2.08	0.8497***	3.08	−0.0638	−2.38
Retired	0.1634	0.84	−0.7226	−1.39	−0.9747***	−2.15	−0.0507	−4.69
Housewife	*		*		0.814***	3.59	0.0345	1.96
Unemployed	0.5603	2.79	0.1352	0.50	1.7353***	11.69	0.0332	2.84
Self-employed	0.1159	0.24	**		0.4387***	1.10	0.0014	0.05
Log equiv. income	−0.3646	−5.45	0.4490	3.40	−0.2341	−3.96	0.0040	1.00
Health index	−0.7259	−2.88	−0.2853	−0.65	0.7837****	2.70	0.1524***	10.68
Unexplained happiness, 95	**0.0365**	−0.65	**−0.0044**	−0.04	**−0.0886**	−1.56	**0.0127**	4.09
Constant	4.0965	4.75	−6.2979	−3.78	−4.4105	−4.06	0.7368	16.09
Observations	3050		1397		4491		4457	
Pseudo R^2	0.0759		0.1541		0.2077		0.0930	

Notes: *Omitted.

**1995 values employed.

***Dropped: perfect predictor.

****The unexpected sign here is a spurious artifact of one of the three questions underlying the health index: 'In the last 30 days did you miss any work or study days due to illness?'

Interestingly enough, education levels also had no effects on the probability of being employed.[22] This most likely reflects the dramatic nature of the economic transition in Russia, and the fact that many highly educated people are either overqualified for what they are doing and/or are unable to find jobs.[23]

Health is one of the most important variables affecting subjective well-being. In our first exploration of the determinants of happiness (discussed in Chapter 3), we find that health—as measured by a neutral index based on a number of questions about days missed due to illness, hospitalization, and so on—is positively and significantly correlated with happiness. (The three questions that made up the index were: In the last 30 days did you miss any work or study days due to illness? Have you been in hospital in the last three months? Have you in the last 30 days had any health problems?)

We then examined the effects of residual or unexplained happiness on our health index. We found that residual happiness had positive and significant effects on health (see Table 4.5). Thus not only does good health make people happier, but our findings suggest that happiness may have additional positive effects on health, something which is often alluded to in the literature, but is more difficult to prove empirically with most data. The same cognitive bias or other attitudinal traits that seem to have positive

---

[22] In order to make sure that this result was not driven by selection bias—say by the few people not eligible for employment in the sample—we reran this same regression with only those employed in 1995, omitting students, retired, and the unemployed in 1995—and got the same results on education.

[23] Another rather interesting result on unemployment is that the health index was positively and significantly correlated with being unemployed in 2000. This may well be the result of spurious correlation, as one question on the index asks 'how many days of work did you miss due to illness?', and obviously unemployed people would answer zero.

effects on individuals' labor market performance may also influence the manner in which they take care of their health. We explore the relationship between happiness and health in greater detail in the subsequent chapter.

Finally, we examined the effects of smoking and drinking. We find that smoking in the year 2000 has a negative and significant correlation with happiness levels. In contrast, quitting smoking—which 257 respondents, or 3% of the sample, did between 1995 and 2000—was positively correlated, and just short of significant at the 5% level, with changes in happiness during the period (but had no effects on happiness levels).[24]

Our index of drinking, a variable that indexes the amount of drinks per week a person consumed in the year 1995, is correlated with happiness in 1995, although the result was insignificant for the same regression with 2000 variables (see Table 4.6). Yet change in drinking, a variable that captures increases in the amount of drinking from 1995 to 2000, was negatively correlated with happiness levels in 2000 (significant at the 10% level). Thus while drinking is positively correlated with happiness, excessive drinking does not seem to be good for well-being.

We then used our residual happiness measure to see if unexplained happiness had any effects on the likelihood of smoking or drinking or of quitting smoking. We found that residual happiness was correlated with our drinking index (significant at the 10% level). In other words, happier people drank more on average than others (and/or some of their more positive attitude is due to their drinking?). Married people also drank more

---

[24] With some specifications this effect was significant at the 5% level, and with others it was just shy of significance at the 5% level.

Table 4.6 Drinking, smoking, and happiness
Dependent variable: happiness (ordered logit regression).

Independent variables	1995 a		2000 b		2000 c	
	Coef.	z	Coef.	z	Coef.	z
Age	−0.1018	−5.38	−0.1177	−7.23	−0.1233	−5.15
Age^2	0.0012	5.53	0.0012	6.64	0.0013	4.90
Male	0.0875	0.90	0.2339	2.51	0.2339	2.09
Married	0.1655	1.70	0.1103	1.24	0.0359	0.34
Log equivalence income	0.3903	8.33	0.3779	7.84	0.3814	6.53
Education level	0.0609	2.37	0.0067	0.26	0.0289	0.93
Minority	0.2425	2.31	0.1872	1.83	0.1148	0.93
Student	0.5517	1.99	−0.1505	−0.76	−0.2954	−0.50
Retired	−0.3959	−2.69	−0.3372	−2.39	−0.2364	−1.43
Housewife	0.0743	0.35	−0.0606	−0.26	0.0495	0.17
Unemployed	−0.3033	−2.10	−0.6749	−5.04	−0.7150	−4.25
Self-employed	0.9336	3.27	0.3546	1.20	0.2809	0.86
Health index	0.4217	2.44	0.4033	2.36	0.5069	2.40
Smoker	−0.2562	−2.70	−0.2615	−2.85	−0.2182	−2.01
Index of drinking	0.0946	2.70	−0.0077	−0.24	*	*
Change in drinking, 95–00	*	*	*	*	−0.0609	−1.87
Observations	2405		2532		2532	
Pseudo R^2	4.0286		0.0299		0.0299	

Notes: * omitted.
Regression a: 1995 happiness, with smoking and drinking variables.
Regression b: 2000 happiness, with smoking and drinking variables.
Regression c: 2000 happiness, with change in drinking (1995–2000) substituted for index of drinking.

than others, suggesting that there is a social interaction effect: people are more likely to drink together than alone.

Residual happiness was not correlated with either starting or quitting smoking, even though people who smoke are less happy, on average (see Table 4.7). Thus while smoking seems to have negative effects on happiness and/or unhappy people are more likely to smoke, we find no

Table 4.7 Effects of happiness on smoking and drinking

Dependent variable:	Quit smoking (given smoker in 1995)		Start smoking (given non-smoker in 1995)		Drinking in 2000			
Condition:								
Regression technique:	a Logit		b Logit		c Ordered logit		d Ordered logit	
Independent variables	Coef.	z	Coef.	z	Coef.	z	Coef.	z
Age	−0.1342	−3.39	−0.0538	−1.60	0.0161	0.92	−0.0203	−0.82
Age²	0.0014	3.31	0.0000	−0.03	−0.0002	−0.99	0.0002	0.88
Male	0.6333	−2.63	1.7698	11.10	1.4992	17.80	1.1276	10.74
Married	−0.0069	−0.07	−0.1909	−2.18	0.1043	2.14	0.0549	0.95
Education level	0.3080	1.45	−0.1173	−0.62	−0.1178	−1.31	−0.1081	−1.01
Minority	0.1427	2.34	−0.0835	−1.43	0.0170	0.65	0.0379	1.20
Student	0.2827	1.24	−0.4233	−2.00	−0.09	−0.87	−0.0359	−0.28
Retired	0.3348	0.26	−0.4082	−1.09	−0.17	−0.55	−0.6432	−1.08
Housewife	0.036	0.10	−0.6679	−1.84	−0.31	−2.12	−0.4731	−2.77
Unemployed	0.7922	1.49	−0.6532	−1.35	−0.16	−0.69	−0.2246	−0.75
Self-employed	0.1334	0.53	0.4872	2.18	0.16	1.20	0.0685	0.42
Log equiv. income	−1.3952	−1.35	0.3464	0.66	0.7154	2.45	0.3681	1.13
Health index	−0.3446	−0.92	−0.3765	−1.06	0.26	1.44	0.16	0.77
Unexplained happiness, 95	**0.0396**	**0.47**	**−0.0023**	**−0.03**	**0.0575**	**1.56**	**0.0176**	**0.41**
	*		*		*	*		
Index of drinking, 95					*		0.5462	12.96
							*	
Constant	0.1769	0.14	1.9562	1.76	*		*	
Observations	1252		3205		2355		1685	
Pseudo R²	0.0351		0.2183		0.0582		0.0868	

Notes: *Omitted.

Regression a: Probability of quitting smoking, given that respondent was a smoker in 1995.

Regression b: Probability of starting smoking, given that respondent was a nonsmoker in 1995.

Regression c: Amount of drinking in 2000 (index 1–6).

Regression d: Amount of drinking in 2000, controlling for amount of drinking in 1995.

causal relationship between unexplained happiness and either starting or stopping smoking. Our insignificant results may well be due to the lack of clarity in terms of causation. Unhappiness might drive people to smoke, but it also could provoke them to change their habits and quit.

Married people, meanwhile, were less likely to *start* smoking than others, while self-employed people were more likely to start. Perhaps marriage acts as a sort of peer effect in preventing people from starting to smoke, while being self-employed has the opposite effect—both working alone and possibly with more pressure. Neither marriage nor self-employment had any effect on quitting smoking, however, perhaps suggesting that quitting smoking—which is undoubtedly harder—is more immune to these kinds of pressures than is starting.

Conclusions

In this chapter, we explored whether happiness had causal properties on future income and other variables, based on panel data for Russia. In other words, while we know that more income (up to a certain level) and stable marital status and more education make people happier, does happiness matter to future outcomes? Does happiness pay? Accepting that the Russian context is an unusual one, our results were intuitive. Happier people earned more income and were healthier, and the role of attitudes was more important for those respondents with less income and assets to leverage their future outcomes.

Psychologists attribute stability in happiness levels over time (analogous to the 'residual' happiness levels that we identify) to positive cognitive bias, such as self-esteem, control, and optimism. Our results suggest that these same factors may affect people's performance in their earnings activities and that these traits have relatively more importance for those at lower levels of income.

We also found that happiness had positive effects on health. We found that happier people drank more on average, but that reducing one's level of drinking also made people happier, suggesting that excessive drinking is not good for happiness. Divorce made people significantly less happy, although unhappier people were not more likely to get divorced. In short, happiness seems to have effects on people's outcomes in the labor market, at the doctor's office, and at the bar. In contrast, divorce affected people's happiness, but unhappiness did not cause divorce.

Our findings about the effects of well-being on future economic performance—in particular that both happiness and high expectations seem to have positive effects on income in future periods and not only the other way around—suggest that better understanding of subjective well-being can contribute to policy questions, such as those concerning labor market performance and concerning health. The results are tempered, however, by the exceptional nature of the time period and country from which they come. An important next stage is to test the broader relevance of these results against those from similar data—to the extent they exist—from other countries.

These results are suggestive and do not establish a clear direction of causality. It is possible that causality runs from policy-relevant variables or factors such as economic performance to happiness, as well as from happiness to economic performance, or from third factors that influence both. What, then, are the implications? Surely that there are factors that influence happiness that can be influenced by policy, and many of these are germane to virtually all country contexts, such as stable employment and marriage, good health, and income levels which are beyond the subsistence level, among others.

To the extent happiness is linked with better future outcomes in the labor and health arenas, our results suggest that increased happiness can have positive externalities that merit the attention of policymakers and scholars of the topic. To the extent that there are third factors that influence happiness and economic performance/health, then a better understanding of the intersection between contextual factors that can be influenced by economic and other policies, and character-related or cognitive traits that are the domain of health practitioners and psychologists, is necessary. While none of these questions will be answered definitively in this book, Chapters 5, 6, and 7 will explore the respective roles of health, economic, and institutional variables in greater detail.

CHAPTER 5

Happiness and Health across Countries and Cultures[1]

In September 1932, the mother superior of the American School Sisters of Notre Dame decided that all new nuns should be asked to write an autobiographical sketch...Of the nuns that were still alive in 1991, only 21% of the most cheerful quarter died in the following nine years, compared with 55% of the least cheerful quarter of the nuns.

American Nuns Study, cited by Layard (2005)

Happiness studies consistently reveal a strong relationship between health and happiness. Indeed, the relationship is more statistically robust than that between happiness and income. Good health is linked to higher levels of happiness, and health shocks—such as serious diseases or permanent disabilities—have negative and often lasting effects on happiness. At the same time, a number of studies find that happier people are healthier. Causality seems to run in both directions, most likely because personality

[1] This chapter draws heavily on Graham (2008a).

traits or other unobservable variables are linked to better health and higher happiness levels.

Happiness studies have exposed paradoxes in the income–happiness relationship. There is some evidence that the happiness–health relationship is non-linear; in other words, advances in health status do not necessarily result in equivalent increases in happiness, particularly as overall health conditions improve. This relationship recalls the Easterlin paradox (discussed in Chapter 1), although we know less about it. Clearly there is adaptation: health standards have been improving over time and people come to expect them. There may also be diminishing marginal returns in some sense: once certain levels of longevity are reached, the benefits of increased longevity may be weighed against other objectives, such as better quality of life during the living years. Even less is known about the happiness–health relationship among the very poor, who typically have lower expectations for health standards and under-report health problems. Happiness surveys offer a new tool for exploring these questions.

Happiness surveys allow us to test whether norms and expectations about health outcomes differ across cohorts and mediate the health–happiness relationship. Our research on obesity, for example, shows that weight norms—and the stigma associated with departing from them—vary significantly across socio-economic and racial cohorts in the United States. Blacks and Hispanics, for example, suffer lower stigma-related obesity costs than do whites (discussed in detail below).[2] These differences may affect individuals' discount rates as they decide whether to 'invest' in healthier behaviors, such as preventing obesity, which requires substantial inter-temporal consumption choices (e.g., eating less and going to the

---

[2] Felton and Graham (2005).

gym more today for better health tomorrow). Our research on divergences between objective and subjective evaluations of health, meanwhile, shows how individuals value and adapt—or not—to different health conditions, and how those valuations are mediated by gender, age, income, reference groups, and friendships, among other variables.

This chapter will review some findings on health and happiness and identify areas where new research could shed light on as yet unanswered health policy challenges. In the end, better understanding of the health–happiness relationship may enhance economists' ability to measure human well-being.

Happiness and Health

Health is recognized to be one of the most important correlates of well-being. Of all the variables in our happiness equations, health status—as gauged by an index of a number of pointed questions on self-reported health—has the strongest coefficient, see Table 5.1. This is consistent with studies in other countries and regions. Higher levels of happiness are also associated with better health outcomes.[3] For example, a recent study in the OECD countries finds that hypertension prevalence and average country-level happiness rankings are negatively correlated (a finding which is not driven by doctor availability). While it is not clear which way the causality runs: happier people may be less disposed to hypertension or hypertension may lead to unhappiness (or both), there is some sort of virtuous happiness and health circle.[4]

---

[3] Dolan (2006).

For the effects of happiness on income and health in Russia, see Graham et al. (2004).

[4] Blanchflower and Oswald (2004).

Table 5.1 Happiness and health

Independent variables	Happiness in the US 1972–1998		Happiness in Latin America 2001		Happiness in Russia 2000	
	Coef.	z	Coef.	z	Coef.	z
Age	−0.025	−5.20	−0.025	−4.21	−0.067	−7.42
Age^2	0.033	7.53	0.000	4.72	0.001	7.15
Male	−0.199	−6.80	−0.002	−0.07	0.152	2.80
Married	0.775	25.32	0.066	1.63	0.088	1.40
Log Income[1]	0.163	9.48	0.395	10.56	0.389	11.48
Education	0.007	1.49	−0.003	−0.64	0.015	0.96
Minority[2]	−0.400	−10.02	−0.083	−2.49	0.172	2.46
Other race	0.049	0.59				
Student	0.291	3.63	0.066	1.01	0.199	1.59
Retired	0.219	3.93	−0.005	−0.06	−0.378	−3.97
Housekeeper	0.065	1.66	−0.053	−1.04	0.049	0.33
Unemployed	−0.684	−3.72	−0.495	−7.54	−0.657	−6.51
Self-employed	0.098	2.29	−0.098	−2.33	0.537	2.23
Health	0.623	35.91	0.468	24.58	0.446	3.82
Pseudo R^2	0.075		0.062		0.033	
Number of obs.	24128		15209		5134	

[1] Log wealth is the variable in the Latin America regression.

[2] Black is the variable in the US regression.

Ordered logit estimation; year dummies included but not shown.

Source: GSS data, Author's calculations.

Ordered logit estimation; country dummies included but not shown.

Source: Latinobarometro, 2001. Author's calculations.

Samples are nationally representative at the country level, but are not weighted for population size for each country. There are roughly 1,000 respondents per country in the survey.

Ordered logit estimation.

Source: Graham et al. (2004).

The dependent variable for all three equations, happiness, is based on answers to the question 'generally speaking, how happy are you with your life?'

Details on scores in the text.

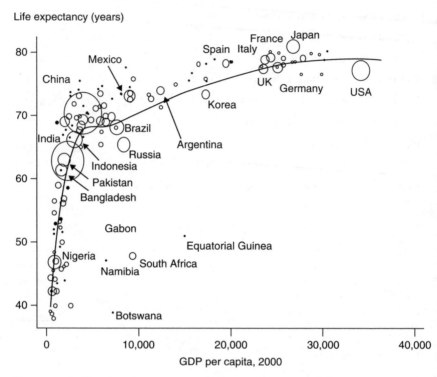

Figure 5.1 Millennium Preston curve: Life expectancy versus GDP

Notes: The circles in the figure represent population sizes for the respective countries.

Health Gains and Happiness: Adaptation, again?

Analogous to the Easterlin paradox, where country-level income matters to happiness more at lower levels of income than at higher ones, the Preston curve shows that income matters much more to health and longevity at lower levels of income than at higher ones, see Figure 5.1.

Income gains in poor countries are associated with rapid improvements in basic health and in defeating preventable diseases and lowering infant mortality rates. The availability of clean water and electricity can make a huge difference in the diarrhoeal diseases that claim so many infant deaths in poor countries.[5] At higher levels of per capita income, technology and scientific innovation play more of a role than income in generating cures for the types of diseases that are more typical of developed economies, such as cancer. Gains in longevity at higher levels of life expectancy, meanwhile, are much harder to achieve. At the same time, due to technological advances, poor countries today are able to enjoy much higher levels of life expectancy at lower income levels than were their predecessors in the development process.[6]

The health and happiness relationship may well reflect these trends, if not exactly mirroring the paradox. People no doubt adapt to better health conditions, and in turn expect them. Angus Deaton finds that satisfaction with health (which is highly correlated with happiness) and per capita income are surprisingly uncorrelated across countries. A higher percentage of Kenyans (82%), for example, are satisfied with their personal health than Americans (81%), and the United States ranks 81st out of 115 countries in public confidence in the health system—lower than countries such as India, Malawi, and Sierra Leone.[7] Once certain levels of health standards and longevity are achieved, there is no consistent cross-country relationship between health and happiness. What that level is remains an open question (as it does for income in the Easterlin paradox). Within countries, however, healthier people are happier—similar to difference in the across and within country relation between income and happiness.

In the same vein, and based on the subsample of 20 Latin American countries in the Gallup World Poll, Eduardo Lora and I find that average

[5] Adrianzen and Graham (1974).
[6] Deaton (2004); Preston (1975).
[7] Deaton (2008).

health satisfaction across countries is uncorrelated with either income levels or health standards across countries. Average health satisfaction is much higher in Guatemala, for example, than in Chile, although both health care availability and health indicators are much higher in the latter.[8] Health satisfaction is positively but weakly correlated with per capita income levels across countries, and negatively correlated with economic growth.[9] It is positively correlated with life expectancy, as one would expect, but also positively correlated with the infant mortality rate, which one would certainly not expect! One reason for this may be a selection bias: even in countries with high levels of infant mortality, those that survive past age five are typically able to lead relatively long lives. The same conditions that lead to high levels of infant mortality—such as poor sanitation and water quality—may lead to chronic disease but not usually to mortality among adults. More generally, though, health satisfaction seems to be more closely correlated with variables that reflect cultural differences rather than with objective health indicators. Within countries, meanwhile, the rich are more satisfied than the poor with their health, but the gap is small—only seven percentage points between the top and bottom quintiles. The gaps in incomes, in objective health indicators, and in access to health care services are much greater than the gaps in satisfaction.

A recent study, based on a subsample of wealthy European countries, finds that happiness and longevity are *negatively* correlated. Health expenditures and happiness are also negatively correlated for this sample. All of the countries in the sample have widely available care. At these

---

[8] See Graham and Lora (forthcoming).

[9] One can imagine any number of factors related to growth, such as longer working hours and/or traffic congestion that could undermine satisfaction with health. See Graham and Lora (forthcoming).

socio-economic levels, where people have come to expect good health, factors other than longevity may mediate the happiness and health relationship, such as norms about health standards. In addition, longevity is only one measure of health, and slightly shorter but healthier life years may matter more to happiness than extending already long life expectancies. Quality of life is likely worse in the latter years, which are typically characterized by a range of chronic health conditions. Similar to income, after a certain point more health may not buy more happiness, and other factors related to quality of life matter more.[10] Meanwhile, it is also possible that, given an overall high standard and widely available health care, less healthy (and less happy) people demand more health expenditures. At the bottom end of the income scale, meanwhile, some countries with extremely poor health standards, such as Guatemala, Honduras, Nigeria, and Pakistan, have relatively high average happiness scores. Yet *within* each set of these same countries, healthier people are happier, again echoing the Easterlin paradox.

The positive relationship between happiness and health tends to be stronger for psychological health than it is for physical health.[11] While serious illness or disability have significant and negative effects on happiness, these individuals often adapt their expectations for health status downwards over time and return—at least partly—to their initial happiness levels. Their reference norms often change to others with the same disease or disability rather than to other healthy individuals.

Individuals suffering from depression, in contrast, are much less likely to experience this kind of adaptation, perhaps because coping mechanisms are weakened by the lower happiness levels that characterize depression.[12] In

[10] On quality-adjusted life years (QALYs), see Broome (1999); Hausman (2007).
[11] Dolan (2006).
[12] Ibid.

research based on US data (discussed below), we find that obese respondents are more likely to report depression than the average, and the causality runs from obesity to reported depression, rather than the other way around.[13] It seems unlikely that they will escape from that depression unless what causes it—obesity—is reversed, a goal which is not easily achieved. In more recent research exploring the variance in the well-being costs of different health conditions (also discussed below), we find that the well-being costs associated with mental illness or with conditions associated with uncertainty, such as pain and anxiety, are much greater than those associated with physical problems, such as mobility and self-care problems, again suggesting that it is more difficult to adapt to psychological than to physical conditions.

Variance in the Health–Happiness Relationship: The Example of Obesity

Norms and expectations of health standards vary a great deal across countries and cohorts within them. This may help explain the lack of a linear relationship between happiness and health across countries. Happiness surveys capture the variance in the well-being 'costs' of different health conditions and, as such, are a tool for detecting this variance. In the case of obesity, for example, norms are quite different across countries and development levels. A century ago in Europe, it was seen as desirable—a sign of prosperity, as it still seems to be in Russia and some developing countries today. And surely norms of appearance vary across cultures as well.

[13] We find that lagged obesity is correlated with depression future periods, while lagged depression is not correlated with future obesity. See Felton and Graham (2005); Graham (2008a).

Our research assesses the well-being costs associated with obesity in the United States and Russia, based on data from the US National Longitudinal Survey of Youth, and the Russian Longitudinal Monitoring Survey. We find that obese people are, on average, less happy than the non-obese. But those well-being costs are mediated by social norms. We find that the unhappiness associated with obesity in the United States is much greater in socio-economic and professional cohorts where obesity is *not* the norm, such as in white-collar professions, and is much lower among poor blacks and Hispanics, where obesity rates are typically higher.[14] These unhappiness costs are additional to the objective health consequences associated with obesity and lower happiness levels. Higher levels of stigma may make people more aware of the health consequences of their condition.

In Russia, in contrast, where obesity rates are highest among wealthy men, we find that the condition is associated with higher happiness levels. The relationship only turns negative at extreme levels of obesity (BMI >33), when the health consequences become more difficult to ignore. At lower levels, there is limited awareness of the health consequences.

Figure 5.2 shows how the impact of obesity on depression varies among demographic groups in the United States. The base impact of obesity on happiness is 0.57; that is, white obese people with income in the middle quintile living in the East in a non-urban area who have not graduated high school are 0.57 standard deviations—in other words, half of the average distance from the standard score—higher on the depression scale than their non-obese counterparts. In contrast, obese people who fit the same demographic characteristics but are in the fourth income quintile are 0.33 (0.57–0.24) standard deviations more depressed than their non-obese

[14] Felton and Graham (2005); Graham (2008a).

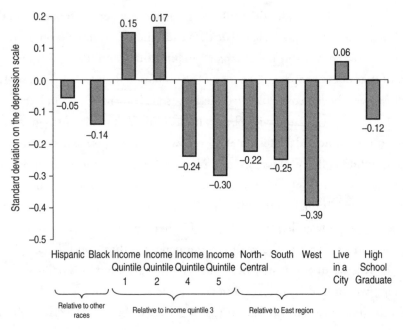

Figure 5.2 Obesity and unhappiness

counterparts. The well-being costs of obesity are highest for low-income whites who live in the East, live in a city, and have not graduated from high school. We posit that obesity serves as a type of physical marker that distinguishes them from wealthier, more educated, higher-status whites. The same norm does not seem to apply to obese blacks and Hispanics in lower income cohorts, where higher obesity rates are the norm.

The well-being costs of obesity are higher for those who depart from the norm for their rank/status cohort. Because obesity prevalence is so much lower in high-status occupations, it likely carries a higher stigma. Other studies find that the perceived discrimination associated with obesity increases with professional status. Norms about appearance seem to be stronger across occupation and status than they are across income and racial groups.

Corroborating these findings on norms, a recent study in the *New England Journal of Medicine* found that the likelihood of being obese increases by 57% if one has a friend who is obese. The effects of friendship are stronger than those of having obese siblings or obese neighbors.[15] These effects are likely due both to lower levels of stigma associated with obesity if one is surrounded by obese friends, as well as to shared behaviors, such as eating and exercise patterns, among the obese and non-obese cohorts.

Oswald and Powdthavee, using data from the United Kingdom, posit that hyperbolic discounting (e.g. difficulty postponing current consumption for future benefit) poses worse problems for affluent societies—as in the case of obesity and widely available cheap food. They find that discounting is mediated by norms: the problem is worse if higher weight norms in your cohort provide additional disincentives to losing weight.[16] They also highlight higher weight norms among lower income cohorts, for whom there are no significant unhappiness costs associated with obesity.

Obesity also brings difficulties in the job market. We find that the obese are 29% less likely than the non-obese to move up an income quintile in any given year; accounting for education, gender, race, and other demographic factors, the obese still are 12% less likely to experience upward mobility. We do not know whether this is due to lower expectations and less effort or to greater job discrimination. We do know that conforming to higher weight norms is condemning a significant part of society to inferior outcomes in both professional and health arenas, as well as lower levels of happiness.

[15] Christakis and Fowler (2007); Graham et al. (2007).
[16] Oswald and Powdthavee (2007).

Table 5.2 Does obesity cause depression or the other way around? Obesity and depression correlations

Only for subjects whose lagged 'extra' BMI >0
(i.e. must be overweight in previous round)
BMI predicts depression

Dependent variable: depression	*OLS*
lagged depression	0.448***
lagged extra BMI	0.024***
constant	−0.168***
Depression doesn't predict BMI	
dependent variable: extra BMI	*OLS*
lagged extra BMI	0.928***
lagged depression	0.04
constant	0.124

Notes: *** indicates significance at the 1% level.

More evidence for the importance of obesity itself, rather than other factors, comes from the fact that causality seems to run from overweight to depression rather than the other way around. Being overweight in one year (e.g. having a positive standard deviation from the mean BMI for your age, income, and professional group) is highly correlated with being depressed in the next year. Being depressed in one year does not seem to be correlated with being overweight the next.[17] Obesity thus has a direct effect on happiness, although it is mediated by other factors, such as the extent of stigma, see Table 5.2.

---

[17] Depression is measured in standard deviations using the Center for Epidemiological Studies depression scale (CESD) variable. The mean is zero and measured over the entire population, not just particular reference groups. Thus if a depression variable reads 1, it is one standard deviation more depressed than the average. Table 5.2 shows that for every extra BMI a respondent had in period 1, they were 0.024 standard deviations more depressed in period 2.

Public health messages based on promoting healthier lifestyles may have little impact on respondents who have higher than average discount rates, due to low expectations for the future and lower incentives to delay consumption and spend income, and effort to exercise. If these same individuals are more likely to be depressed, the health messages will be even less effective.

Poverty, Health, and Happiness

We have limited understanding of the health–happiness relationship among the very poor, both in the United States and beyond. The very poor are notorious for under-reporting health problems, not least because they rarely stay home from work when they are ill. One possibility is that health shocks have less of a negative effect on their reported happiness because their expectations for good health are lower. Alternatively, health problems— either for individuals or for members of their household—increase the income insecurity of the poor, who rarely have insurance or access to good medical care. Insecurity is associated with lower happiness levels.[18] Having a sick household member typically sacrifices the wage of an income earner, who has no choice but to stay at home to provide care. At the same time, the costs of medicines can be deleterious to poor households.

In Latin America, we find that respondents who have access to health insurance are happier than the average, as well as older, wealthier, more educated, and more likely to be married. As in the case of being able to insure against future income shocks by saving, the ability to insure against

---

[18] Bannerjee and Duflo (2007); Graham and Pettinato (2002a).

future health shocks seems to have positive effects on happiness above and beyond those of wealth and education levels.[19]

The very poor lack access to insurance, and rely primarily on informal social networks. Yet these networks are limited in their ability to protect against major health shocks, which result in forgone earnings and expenditure drops. Gertler and Gruber find that in Indonesia a decline in the health index of the household head is associated with a fall in non-medical expenditures. In India, large expenditures on health ($70 and higher) are covered by borrowing or dis-saving, which can take the form of the children leaving school. These same households are the least likely to get medical treatment in the case of illness.[20]

Banerjee, Duflo, and Deaton, based on surveys from India, find that the poor report being under a great deal of financial and psychological stress. Case and Deaton have similar findings for India, South Africa, and the United States. The most frequently cited reason cited for stress is health problems (29% of respondents). At the same time, reported happiness is not particularly low. The authors, like others, find that the poor do not in general complain about their health or about life in general.[21]

An obvious challenge for this line of research is understanding if poor health is not fully reflected in the poor's responses to happiness surveys because they have low expectations or are unaware that better standards are possible, or whether the health–happiness relationship is truly different (e.g. has a different slope) when health standards are materially lower.

An analogous challenge exists in the income–happiness relationship—the so-called 'happy peasant' problem discussed in Chapter 6. It is impossible

[19] Regression results available from the authors.
[20] Gertler and Gruber (2002).
[21] Bannerjee and Duflo (2007); Case and Deaton (2005); Deaton (2004).

to compare the response of a peasant who is destitute and likely to live a short and disease-ridden life, but reports that they are very happy (due to a cheery disposition or lack of awareness of a better lifestyle), with that of a millionaire who is likely to lead a much longer and healthier life but reports that they are miserable (due to unrealistic aspirations or to comparison effects with even wealthier neighbors). We find that in rapidly growing developing economies, it is upwardly mobile, lower middle income respondents rather than the poor who are made unhappy by inequality or economic insecurity, due to higher levels of awareness and to loss aversion.[22]

Trends across countries, which show obesity rates rising as countries become more affluent, provide general support for the proposition that health and weight norms can shift in the same way aspirations about income levels change. Public health trends in Latin America are a case in point. While severe malnutrition was prevalent in the region decades ago, incidence has decreased significantly, and obesity and complex nutritional problems are now the primary concerns of public health experts.[23] Whether the obese in the region are happier, as in Russia, or less so, as in the United States, is a research question.

Better understanding the effects that aspirations and awareness have on responses to happiness surveys remains a challenge for happiness research and for understanding the relationship between happiness and health. We do not have sufficient data at present to explore how or if the health and happiness relationship differs among the poor, and if the difference is driven by levels (e.g. differences in basic health levels and expectations

---

[22] Graham and Pettinato (2002a).

[23] Author's participation in the Scientific Advisory Board of the Nutrition Research Institute in Lima, Peru. For a discussion of how modest changes in mean weight can shift the overall norm up, see Hammond and Epstein (2007).

about them) or by the slope (e.g. do improvements in basic health generate more results in terms of happiness at higher levels of income than at lower ones?). Targeted studies could enhance our understanding of the mediating variables, how changing norms and standards affect that relationship, and the factors which could encourage the poor (and their governments) to make better investments in health.

Inequality

Inequality, which is related to but distinct from poverty, plays a role in the happiness–health relationship. Michael Marmot's (2004) famous study of British civil servants finds that relative status is linked to health outcomes, with higher status civil servants having longer and healthier lives than lower status ones. He attributes these findings to higher levels of stress, in addition to the complex relationship between income, status, and well-being.

Our own research finds that inequality—proxied by relative income differences from the national mean—has negative effects on happiness in contexts where inequality is high and persistent, such as Latin America. Inequality can also generate perverse incentives—which raise discount rates and discourage the poor from saving and investing in their and their children's future.[24] A remaining question is whether these incentives affect the health investments of the poor, by making them less likely to set aside the time and resources required to invest in their and their children's health, thereby exacerbating poverty traps and further reducing well-being.

[24] Graham and Felton (2006a).

How Different Illnesses Affect Your Life: Some Evidence from Well-Being Surveys and EQ-5D Scores for Latin America

The EQ-5D or Euro-Quality 5 Dimensions questionnaire is a subjective health assessment tool that is very closely linked to objective health indicators. The EQ-5D asks respondents if they suffer from the five conditions listed below, with the possible answers being: (a) no; (b) moderate; and (c) extreme; only one answer is allowed per dimension. The dimensions are: (a) problems with mobility (your ability to walk around); (b) problems with self-care (your ability to take care of yourself); (c) problems with the usual acts (work, study, housework, family, or leisure activities); (d) pain; and (e) anxiety.

The original EQ-5D studies were conducted in the United States and Europe. More recently, we were able to generate a unique data set via the Latin America subset of the Gallup World Poll, in which the EQ-5D question was included along with the usual life and health satisfaction questions for a sample of almost 20,000 respondents.[25] That data set allowed us a new method for valuing health states—via life and health satisfaction scores—that is arguably less biased and more robust than directly asking individuals suffering from various conditions how they are affected by those conditions. Our results, reported below, highlight the negative effects of conditions that are related to uncertainty and anxiety, as opposed to those of physical conditions such as reduced mobility, which individuals seem to adapt to more easily.

A major contribution of the original EQ-5D analysis was to shed light on how individuals value different health states or, put another way, the well-being costs of various ailments. The original EQ-5D studies were conducted

---

[25] For detail, see Graham et al. (2009).

in the United Kingdom; they were later implemented in the United States. The UK study, led by Dolan (1997), covered 2,997 respondents in England, Scotland, and Wales in 1993.[26] The US study, led by Shaw et al. (2005), was conducted in 2002 and was based on a 12,000 respondent, nationally representative sample.[27] A dimension for which there is no problem was assigned a level 1, while a dimension with extreme problems was assigned a level 3. Each health state described by the instrument had a five-digit descriptor, ranging from 11111 for perfect health to 33333 for the worst possible state. The resulting descriptive system defined 243 (5 to the power of 3) health states.[28]

Health state *preferences*, based on a time trade-off method, were then developed for each context by the same authors. The preference rankings were based on interviews using the time trade-off method for a representative subsample of the respondents in each case. In the time trade-offs method, individuals were asked to describe their own health using the EQ-5D description system, and then to rate their health state on a 0 to 100 scale, with 0 being the worst imaginable health state and 100 being the best imaginable health state They were asked to value 13 of the possible health states (rather than 243), using a props method: a set of health state cards and a two-sided time board, one for states considered better than death and one for states considered worse than death. The 13 were 12 EuroQol (EuroQuality

[26] See Dolan (1997).

[27] The study initially oversampled blacks and Hispanics, to ensure adequate representation of minorities. See Shaw et al. (2005).

[28] The designers of the EQ-5D emphasize that it is not without flaws. It emphasizes physical conditions over mental ones, for example. People typically imagine that mental health problems are less bad than they actually are, and that physical health problems are worse than they actually are. Despite these imperfections, the EQ-5D is one of the better objective measures that we have.

five dimensions index) states plus unconscious, based on the assumption that respondents could not realistically evaluate a higher number of states; the selection of states was based on the range of responses and interactions among them.[29] Econometric analysis was then used to determine the relative weights to assign to these preferences.

Respondents were asked time trade-offs values for time spent in various states (e.g. either losing or gaining time spent in full health; the smallest possible time that an individual could choose to spend in a health state was 0.25 years, and the total time period was 10 years, with 5 years being the middle value offered for full health). Values for worse than death states were transformed and bounded by 0 and -1, with the lowest possible health state being -39, which occurred when 0.25 years in a given state followed by 9.75 years in full health was considered equal to death.[30]

Regression results based on the United Kingdom's responses demonstrate that *any* move away from full health was associated with a substantial welfare or well-being loss. The largest welfare loss for a move from level 1—no problems—to level 2—moderate problems—was in the category of pain or discomfort, an effect which was four times greater than that for a corresponding move on the usual activities dimension. Pain or discomfort continued to dominate the weighting for level 3, although mobility level 3 (confined to bed) was given a somewhat similar weight. For the mobility, pain or discomfort, and anxiety or depression dimensions, the move from level 2 to level 3 caused a much greater loss in utility than did the move from level 1 to level 2.[31] Thus extreme conditions, as well as pain in general, seemed to have the strongest (negative) effects on well-being.

[29] The authors thank Paul Dolan for explaining this selection process.

[30] Shaw et al. (2005).

[31] For a more detailed discussion of both methodology and results, see Dolan (1997).

We conducted an additional analysis of the EQ-5D variable for our sample of Latin American respondents in the Gallup Poll, where we compared the valuations based on the traditional time trade-offs valuations with the coefficients on life and health satisfaction, both on the EQ-5D index in general, and on its specific components.

We took advantage of having a unique data set combining subjective evaluations of life and health satisfaction, on the one hand, and health conditions as measured by the EQ-5D, on the other, to study discrepancies between the two measures, and how or if these discrepancies were mediated by socio-demographics, such as age, gender, and income, by reference groups, and by cultural and other norms. We also explored the variance across the particular conditions. We then compared our results to those for the United States and United Kingdom, based on the EQ-5D and time trade-offs methods.

The EQ-5D was an extremely strong predictor of health satisfaction, as well as a good although less strong predictor of life satisfaction (to some extent, though, the causality might run in both directions—happier people may be less likely to report or suffer from various ailments, particularly psychological ones). Our analysis supported the conclusions of the original EQ-5D studies, which point to the importance of any move away from full health. Our work on the individual components highlighted the relative importance of pain, anxiety, and difficulties with usual activities in particular.

Values based on the overall EQ-5D index, as opposed to its individual components, were typically higher than those based on the extreme conditions. A small number of respondents report extreme conditions, and thus they have less weight in the analysis when included separately. The composite index in contrast gives additional weight to the

Table 5.3 Life satisfaction costs of EQ-5D components
Basic results

	Health satisfaction 0–10		Life satisfaction 0–10	
	(1)	(2)	(3)	(4)
EQ-5D index	5.188***		1.436***	
Mobility moderate		−0.460***		0.086
Mobility extreme		−0.032		0.091
Self-care moderate		−0.142		0.157
Self-care extreme		−0.236		0.281
Usual activities moderate		−0.690***		−0.230*
Usual activities extreme		−1.136*		−0.498
Pain moderate		−1.016***		−0.135
Pain extreme		−2.143***		−0.477**
Anxiety moderate		−0.480***		−0.303***
Anxiety extreme		−0.883***		−0.786***
Observations	8249	8249	8250	8250
Countries	17	17	17	17

Notes: *** p<0.01, ** p<0.05, * p<0.1.

extreme conditions, thereby accentuating their importance. The values for life and health satisfaction were much closer for the aggregate index than they were for the components, meanwhile, while the individual components had much higher values for health satisfaction. These latter findings suggest that the composite index is better at capturing the overall effects of health in general, while the components attenuate the effects of particular conditions on satisfaction with health rather than life satisfaction.

We calculated life satisfaction equivalents for the particular components, and found that compared to a baseline per capita household income of $93.7 (PPP adjusted), the average respondent in Latin America would need to be compensated 2.1 times the average monthly income for moderate problems

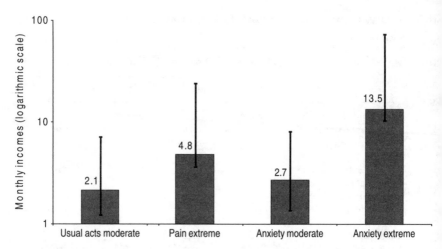

Figure 5.3 Income equivalences of health conditions in EQ-5D (in monthly incomes; comparison income: US$ 93.7 PPP)

Source: Author's calculations based on Gallup 2006 and 2007.

Note: Direct equivalences are based on the effect of each health component on life satisfaction. The EQ5 equivalences are based on the effect of changes in the EQ-5D index, derived from changes in each health component. Vertical bars represent a 95% confidence interval.

with the usual acts, and 2.7 times for moderate anxiety. Extreme pain was more 'expensive' in life satisfaction terms: almost 5 times average income, while extreme anxiety was the most 'expensive': 13.5 times, see Figures 5.3.

Both our findings and those based on time trade-offs methods highlight the importance of pain and anxiety over those of mobility and self-care, albeit with different weights. People's priors tend to be that physical conditions will be worse than they actually are, and that mental conditions are less serious than they actually are. Thus when they actually experience them, they are mediated by these expectations, and the effects of the former are weaker than expected and those of the latter are stronger.

Health and life satisfaction questions are less framed than time trade-offs (TTO) questions. The former may be more effective at picking up the psychological effects of these conditions than are the TTO questions, which are more framed by the particulars of the conditions. At the same time, those same psychological conditions can influence life and health satisfaction responses, biasing them towards more negative assessments. While TTO methods could be influenced by similar biases, it is hard to tell in what direction. While less happy (more anxious) people answer both life and health satisfaction questions more negatively, it is not clear that less happy, more anxious people value healthy life years versus ill life years differently than happier people do.

Our findings highlight the importance of mental illness and of conditions that create uncertainty (pain, anxiety, and difficulties with usual activities), while most people would predict that physical conditions would have stronger negative effects. We also feel that the method of combining different kinds of assessments, while far from perfect, contributes to our understanding of the welfare effects of health. In addition to the usual effects of income levels on both life and health satisfaction, we found some modest differences across age, gender, and income cohorts. The elderly, for example, seem to cope better than the average with mobility/self-care problems, but worse than the average with anxiety.

We found much more of a difference in the impact that various conditions have on health and life satisfaction than the difference in effects of the conditions across cohorts. In particular, there was almost no difference across income groups. The weak effects that we find on income support our earlier findings on health perceptions, where again income plays a surprisingly small role relative to other factors in determining health satisfaction.

Our methodological contributions can also inform health policy. Individuals seem to be better at adapting to health shocks that lead to a one time change—such as a loss in mobility—than they are to conditions which are associated with constant uncertainty, such as pain and anxiety. The appropriate balance of investments in physical versus mental health is a question that must be resolved at the level of particular cultures and societies. Yet our findings suggest that better understanding the causes of anxiety, and how anxiety varies across cohorts, countries, and cultures, might go a long way towards improving health and well-being in general. The strong negative effects of uncertainty in conditions rather than one time shocks might also affect how we think about and/or calculate policy relevant measures, such as quality-adjusted life years (QALYs).

Our findings also highlight the role of comparison effects on health evaluations. The effect of a reference group mean EQ-5D score, as defined by gender, age, area of residence, and education level, was positive and significant on health satisfaction (controlling for own and reference group income), see Table 5.4. This is an important contrast with the usual reference group effects of income: comparison effects in the income domain tend to be negative (due to greed and envy?). In contrast, it is possible that comparisons in the health arena provide more positive signals. As is noted in Chapter 5, there seem to be a number of positive spillover effects on well-being that come from friendships and other social networks; it may be an area where there is an interaction between positive (or negative) psychological and physical effects.

At the least, it suggests that most people do not react to health standards or changes the same way that they do to income standards or changes. While rapid income growth, for example, is often associated with unhappiness, uncertainty, and anxiety among some cohorts, better health seems more likely to produce positive signals. For example, it is more enjoyable to be surrounded by healthy people, while being surrounded by people with

Table 5.4 Friendships and health

Reference groups results

	Health satisfaction 0–10				Life satisfaction 0–10			
	(1)	(2)	(3)	(4)	(5)	(6)	(7)	(8)
1 if has friends			0.158**	0.156**			0.447***	0.438***
Log, monthly per capita household income, US$ PPP	0.169***	0.147***	0.164***	0.143***	0.308***	0.288***	0.297***	0.280***
EQ-5D index	5.277***	5.335***	5.259***	5.317***	1.575***	1.556***	1.488***	1.469***
Mean EQ-5D, education reference group	0.630*	0.654*	0.59	0.198	0.309	0.37	0.323	−0.207
Mean income, education reference group		0.175***		0.166***		0.179***		0.158**
Observations	7725	7572	7684	7532	7725	7572	7684	7532
Reference groups	992	1600	992	1600	993	1601	993	1601
Countries	17	17	17	17	17	17	17	17

Notes: ***p<0.01, **p<0.05, *p<0.1

ill health often risks contagion, among other negative externalities. One possible implication—which needs further exploration—is the extent to which public health investment has community-level spillover effects in terms of more positive attitudes about health. Finally, the interaction between reference group health and attitudes about health again suggests an important role for norms of health in explaining cross-country differences in health policies and outcomes.

In sum, our work based on the EQ-5D and life and health satisfaction indices suggests that standard valuations of health conditions may overestimate the effects of physical conditions, and underestimate those of conditions which are associated with uncertainty and unpredictability, as well as mental illnesses, such as extreme anxiety. Individuals seem better able to adapt to a one time health shock than they are to less extreme but constantly changing conditions. We find that being surrounded by friends or neighbors with better health has positive effects on health satisfaction. Thus broader investments in public health may have positive but not easily observable externalities.

Relevance to Policy?

Happiness studies can help us understand the relationship between happiness and health, and may well provide important information for policy. But, as in the case of happiness and policy more generally, caution is necessary in directly inferring policy applications from these findings. First of all, given that human beings suffer from hyperbolic discounting, it is not obvious that policies that are optimal from a public health standpoint would make people happier. Take, for example, a ban on junk food. While it might have good health consequences, it might decrease the happiness of many individuals—some of whom are not overweight and enjoy junk food.

Second, the issue of adaptation and expectations is an important part of the equation and norms of health vary tremendously across countries and cultures and cohorts within them. People with lower expectations for good health care are less likely to demand it—and indeed may instead be more likely to pursue damaging behaviors such as alcohol and tobacco abuse. Thus, increased provision of health care might not improve their happiness in the short term. Does that mean that those individuals should not have access to better quality care? Those with higher standards are more likely to demand more care, reminding us of the miserable millionaire (or the healthy and unhappy Europeans) and the happy peasant. When expectations are sufficiently high, even increased levels of care may not have any effect on happiness.

Third, our findings on the effects of different health conditions suggest that it is more difficult to adapt to conditions associated with uncertainty, such as pain and anxiety, than to negative but one time physical shocks, such as mobility problems. It is also possible that less happy people are more likely to suffer the effects of pain and anxiety (or to be less able to adapt)—causality conundrums which may overemphasize the negative effects of these conditions. While our work on obesity (based on longitudinal data) suggests that the predominant effect is from obesity to unhappiness and not the other way around, we do not have similar data with which to test our findings on the health and life satisfaction effects of different health conditions.

Finally, as in other domains, the definition of happiness or even health satisfaction matters to its relevance to health policy. While the lack of an imposed definition is what makes happiness surveys a power tool for research across countries and cultures, the same may not hold for policy. Happiness defined as contentment in the Benthamite sense, for example, does not seem like an appropriate objective for health policy; a very overweight child in the United States or a peasant with no access to health care in Guatemala may be very content in the short term—and report high levels of health satisfaction—even though both conditions could lead to very poor long-run health outcomes. Perhaps the most useful—and policy-relevant—information is in better understanding why these respondents are satisfied or happy in the absence of better health care.

In the end, this chapter introduces more questions than it can answer. It highlights the importance of health for happiness and of happiness for health, and suggests that happiness surveys can be a powerful tool for understanding a range of public health behaviors, and in particular adaptation to both good and bad health conditions. Making progress in these areas may ultimately give both happiness and health a more important role in the measurement of human welfare and in policies to enhance it. In the meantime, the following chapters will take up the issue of adaptation to a host of other conditions—both good and bad—in greater detail.

CHAPTER 6

Economic Growth, Crises, Inequality, and More

Mill wrote: 'Men do not desire to be rich but to be richer than other men.'   **Pigou** (1920)

Chapter 2 described the income–happiness relationship and the reasons why it is so complex. Chapter 3 demonstrated some remarkable consistencies in the determinants of happiness across countries of very different levels of development. Chapter 4 found evidence that happiness may also have effects on outcomes of interest, such as labor market performance and income, as well as health. Chapter 5 explored the role of health in greater detail. As discussed in Chapter 2, some of the complexities in the income–happiness relationship are methodological and related to question framing and related issues. Some are empirical and related to the sample of countries and time frame chosen for study. But perhaps some of the most interesting—and still unexplained factors—relate to the nature of economic growth and the generation of income, as well as to the institutional framework that mediates that process.

145

There are large country-level differences in these trends. Many of them are difficult to observe or measure precisely. Comparing institutional frameworks and/or the effects of macro-level trends such as growth on individual welfare are fraught with methodological and other challenges. Accepting those challenges, in this chapter we review what we know about the effects of the nature and pattern of growth on well-being; the role of inequality, inflation and unemployment (the so-called misery index); and the effects of deep crisis on well-being. In the subsequent chapter, we look at political and institutional arrangements, as well as the role that cross-country (and city) differences in crime and corruption play in influencing well-being, with a particular focus on the extent to which people adapt to both good and bad equilibriums. While we cannot precisely measure the effects of all of these variables on the income–happiness relationship, we can at least explore the channels through which they influence it.

Economic Growth: An Unhappy Paradox

The relationship between happiness and income may be affected as much by the pace and nature of income change as it is by absolute levels. Based on the Gallup World Poll in 122 countries around the world, Eduardo Lora and collaborators find that countries with higher levels of per capita GDP have, on average, higher levels of happiness. Yet controlling for levels, they find that individuals in countries with positive growth rates have lower happiness levels. In related joint work, Lora and I chose to call this negative correlation between economic growth and happiness the 'paradox of unhappy growth'.[1]

[1] See Lora and Chaparro (forthcoming); Stevenson and Wolfers (2008). It is also possible that initially happier countries grew faster than initially unhappy countries with the same

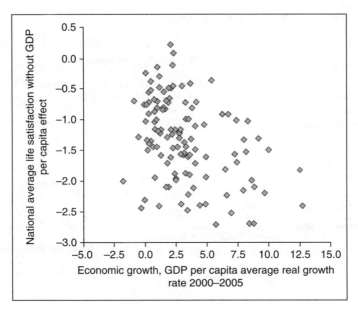

Figure 6.1 The relationship between satisfaction and economic growth
Source: IADB (2008).

A simple scatter plot shows that the relationship between per capita incomes and life satisfaction (as measured by the best possible life question) is linear (when incomes are logged), while that between growth rates and life satisfaction is negative, see Figure 6.1. Econometric analysis confirms the visual relationship in the scatter plot. In an ordinary least squares (OLS) regression with average life satisfaction in each of the 122 countries in the Gallup World Poll as the dependent variable, they find that the coefficient on

income (because they had happier, more productive workers?) and thus the coefficient on growth in a regression which compares the two with final income and final happiness is negative. I thank Charles Kenny for raising this point.

147

Table 6.1 The paradox of unhappy growth

The relationship among satisfaction, income per capita and economic growth

	122 countries	
	GDP per capita[1]	Economic growth[2]
Life satisfaction[3]	0.788***	−0.082***
Standard of living	0.108***	−0.018***
Health satisfaction	0.017*	−0.017***
Job satisfaction	0.077***	−0.006
Housing satisfaction	0.084***	−0.006

Notes: [1] OLS regression; dependent variable is average life satisfaction per country, growth rates are averaged over the past five years. N=122.

[2] The coefficients on GDP per capita are marginal effects; how much does the satisfaction of two countries differ when one has twice the income of another. The coefficients on growth imply how much an additional percentage point of growth affects life satisfaction.

[3] The life satisfaction variable is on a zero to ten scale; all others are the percentage of respondents that are satisfied.

Sources: *IDB—RES us/ng Gallup World Poll 2006–2007 data*. Eduardo Lora. *'Beyond Facts: Understanding Quality of Life in Latin America and the Caribbean'* IADB.

GDP per capita is positive, while that on economic growth—defined as the average rate of growth over the past five years—is negative (and significant in both cases), see Table 6.1. Deaton, and Stevenson and Wolfers, also find evidence of an unhappy growth effect based on the full sample of the Gallup World Poll. Stevenson and Wolfers find insignificant effects of growth in general, but strong negative effects for the first stages of growth in 'miracle' growth economies, such as Ireland and South Korea during their take-off stages. The negative effect becomes insignificant in later stages.[2] Deaton finds that the inclusion of region dummies make a major difference to the results, with the significance being taken up by Africa and Russia, regions which are both fast growing and very unhappy.

[2] Deaton (2008); Stevenson and Wolfers (2008).

In Lora's sample, economic growth is also negatively correlated with perceived standard of living and with health satisfaction. When the sample is split into rich and poor countries (above and below median income), the effect holds for the rich but not for the poor countries. The only variable that is significantly and negatively correlated with growth for the poor country subsample is health satisfaction. One can imagine the factors associated with structural change and rapid growth rates in poor countries—such as long working hours and new industries without provision for worker safety or environmental externalities—that could have negative effects on health. Meanwhile growth is negatively correlated with economic, health, job, and housing satisfaction, in addition to life satisfaction for the rich countries.[3] When the sample is split into above and below median growth rates, the unhappy growth effect only holds for those that are growing at rates above the median.

Soumya Chattopadhyay and I, using Latinobarometro data, also find hints of an unhappy growth effect, or at least an irrelevant growth effect, see Table 6.2. In contrast to Lora et al., we use individual rather than average country happiness on the left-hand side, with the usual socio-demographic and economic controls and clustering the standard errors at the country level. When we include the current GDP growth rate in the equation, as well as the lagged growth rate from the previous year (controlling for levels), we find that the effects of growth rates—and lagged growth rates—are, for the most part, negative but insignificant.[4]

---

[3] This finding based on reported well-being departs from Ben Friedman's more general proposition that some growth is necessary for overall welfare, even as levels increase, in order to keep economies and societies from stagnating and to generate productivity increases and technological advance. See Friedman (2005).

[4] Graham and Chattopadhyay (2008b).

Table 6.2 Happiness immune to country-level economic growth?
Dependent variable: happy.

age	−0.0240	−0.0230	−0.0230	−0.0220
	(4.40)**	(4.34)**	(4.23)**	(4.29)**
age^2	0.0000	0.0000	0.0000	0.0000
	(3.53)**	(3.88)**	(3.72)**	(3.76)**
gender	0.0330	0.0070	0.0070	0.0070
	−1.5500	−0.4800	−0.5200	−0.4800
married	0.0790	0.0910	0.0940	0.0930
	−1.7800	(2.40)*	(2.56)*	(2.60)**
edu	−0.0410	−0.0260	−0.0280	−0.0260
	−1.5300	−1.1800	−1.2900	−1.2800
edu^2	0.0010	0.0010	0.0010	0.0010
	−0.8800	−0.7000	−0.7900	−0.7600
socecon	0.2110	0.2160	0.2150	0.2170
	(5.22)**	(5.76)**	(5.77)**	(5.78)**
subinc	0.2900	0.2900	0.2940	0.2920
	(8.78)**	(8.02)**	(8.36)**	(8.41)**
ceconcur	0.2340	0.2260	0.2360	0.2370
	(9.04)**	(9.50)**	(7.66)**	(8.92)**
unemp	−0.1810	−0.1760	−0.1900	−0.1880
	(2.05)*	(3.45)**	(3.59)**	(3.69)**
poum	0.1800	0.1890	0.1830	0.1840
	(4.48)**	(5.42)**	(5.56)**	(5.59)**
domlang	0.5380	0.4810	0.4840	0.4810
	(2.73)**	(2.48)*	(2.48)*	(2.48)*
vcrime	−0.1160	−0.1060	−0.1060	−0.1080
	(2.30)*	(2.98)**	(2.89)**	(3.08)**
els	0.0900			
	(5.48)**			
growth_gdp	0.0170	−0.0090	−0.0040	−0.0060
	−0.5300	−1.1100	−0.6000	−0.7700
gini	−0.0170	−0.0270	−0.0240	−0.0240
	−0.7000	−1.2400	−1.1200	−1.1900
gdpgrl[1]			−0.0190	−0.0180
			−1.4000	−0.9900
gdpvol[2]				0.0030
				−0.1400
Observations	34808	67308	67308	67308

Notes: Absolute value of z statistics in parentheses.
* significant at 5%; ** significant at 1%.
Regressions clustered at a country level.

It may well be that this unhappy growth is driven by its nature in rapidly changing economies, where growth is often accompanied by changes in rewards to different skill sets and increased job insecurity for some groups, and by related increases in vertical or horizontal inequality. Latin America in recent decades certainly fits this pattern, which may help explain unexpected pockets of frustration in relatively prosperous countries like Chile. Rapid growth in newly reforming economies, meanwhile, as in the case of Korea and Ireland, and in the case of many more recent examples in the emerging market economies, is typically even more uneven in terms of rewards. Cross-country analysis of the income–happiness relationship usually captures some sample of countries in this particular stage of development, and thus the unhappy growth paradox may help explain at least some of the outliers in the analysis.

The Happy Peasants and Frustrated Achievers

There is an overall happiness and income relationship within countries, and wealthier people are, on average, happier than poor people. Yet the within-country story is more complicated than the averages suggest, as in the case of the cross-country income and happiness relationship. It is typically not the poorest people who are most frustrated or unhappy with their conditions or the services that they have access to, for example. Stefano Pettinato and I, based on research in Peru and Russia, identified a phenomenon that is now termed the 'happy peasant and frustrated achiever' problem.[5] This is an apparent paradox, where very poor and destitute respondents report

[5] For more detail, see Graham and Pettinato (2002b).

high or relatively high levels of well-being, while much wealthier ones with more mobility and opportunities report much lower levels of well-being and greater frustration with their economic and other situations. This may be because the poor respondents have a higher natural level of cheerfulness or because they have adapted their expectations downwards. The wealthier and more upwardly mobile respondents, meanwhile, have constantly rising expectations (or are naturally more curmudgeon-like).[6] And a third explanation is also possible: that more driven and frustrated people are more likely to seek to escape situations of static poverty (via channels such as migration), but even when they achieve a better situation, they remain more driven and frustrated than the average. Some combination of all three explanations could indeed be at play.

Regardless of the balance between objective conditions and individual character traits driving the paradox, it mirrors some of the puzzles in the cross-country relationship. These include the apparent greed effect that Deaton finds at the highest income levels, where the slope in the income–happiness relationship is steepest, and the relatively large number of unusually happy countries at the bottom of the income distribution.[7]

A closer look at Pettinato's and my frustrated achievers shows that they were more likely to have had upward mobility than the average, and they were of average incomes and education for their relative samples, of similar

[6] Javier Herrera, for example, using panel data for Peru and Madagascar, finds that people's expectations adapt upwards during periods of high growth and downwards during recessions, and that this adaptation is reflected in their assessments of their life satisfaction (Herrera and Roubaud 2005). People are less likely to be satisfied with the status quo when expectations are adapting upwards. Recent work on China by Whyte and Hun (2006) confirms the direction of these findings.

[7] Deaton (2008).

gender, and more likely to be living in urban than rural areas. Yet they reported that their current economic situation was worse or much worse than the past. And when compared with upwardly mobile respondents who did not report frustration, they had lower levels of general life satisfaction, they had higher fear of unemployment, and they were more concerned about relative income differences (as assessed by their scores on the poor to rich ladder question). Some of this may be driven by less optimistic character traits or lower innate set points, which likely have a similar distribution across most population samples; for example, the percentage of natural curmudgeons is likely similar, regardless of what the dependent variable is. Yet we also posit that at least some of it is contextually driven, not least because of the nature of the contexts under study.

The behavioral economics literature highlights the extent to which individuals value losses disproportionately to gains. It is not a stretch of the imagination to assume that upwardly mobile respondents who managed to escape poverty or near poverty in the volatile macroeconomic context of both Peru and Russia in the late 1990s would be loss averse, not least because of the absence of any safety net or social insurance system. Their income mobility, while having an overall positive trajectory, may have been punctuated with spells of unemployment or unstable income flows. If they were recent migrants, meanwhile, they also likely left strong family or other support networks behind, which are not readily available in crowded urban or peri-urban contexts.

The poor, some of whom rely on subsistence agriculture rather than earnings, have much less income to lose and have likely adapted to constant insecurity. Some of the literature on job insecurity, for example, shows that reported insecurity is actually higher among more formal sector workers with more stable jobs than it is among informal sector workers. The latter have either adapted to higher levels of income and employment insecurity (and/or have selected into jobs with less stability but more freedom).[8]

John Knight and Ramani Gunatilaka, and Martin Whyte and Chunping Hun, each find an analogous urban effect in China, where urban migrants are materially much better off than they were in their pre-migration stage, yet they report higher levels of frustration with their material situation. Once they migrate, their reference norm quickly becomes other urban residents rather than their previous peers in rural areas.[9] In addition to comparison effects, there may also be new costs related to urban living which erode the positive effects of income gains.

The same literature highlights the extent to which individuals adapt much more to income gains than to status gains. Based on the German socio-economic panel, Rafael di Tella and Robert Mac Culloch show that most individuals adapt to a significant income gain or salary increase within a year (in econometric terms, the effect of income gains become insignificant after a one-year lag), while status gains (such as a promotion) have a positive effect that lasts up to five years.[10] In the context of the frustrated achievers in very volatile emerging markets contexts, where currencies are often shifting in value and where the rewards to particular skill and education sets are in flux, as are social welfare systems, income gains may seem particularly ephemeral.

More generally, the paradox highlights the extent to which slightly raised expectations in the context of rapid economic change may result in more frustration and risk aversion than do static poverty levels. To the extent that there are macro-level implications to this micro-level phenomenon,

[8] IADB (2008).
[9] Knight and Gunatilaka (2007); Whyte and Hun (2006).
[10] Di Tella and MacCulloch (2006).

it supports a scenario where growth rates and economic development are associated with less rather than more happiness, at least in the short term, until higher income levels are stabilized. Over the long term, however, there does seem to be a generalized levels effect, with countries with higher levels of gross national product (GNP) on average happier than poorer ones, albeit with a great deal of variance within the subsets of rich and poor countries.

The Aspirations Paradox

A third, related paradox is the 'aspirations paradox'. This paradox is most evident in the health satisfaction arena, although there are also some hints of it in the findings on education, job, and financial satisfaction. Across countries, there is higher tolerance for poor health in the poorer countries, and less satisfaction with better health in the rich ones. Within countries, while rich people are slightly more satisfied with their health than poor ones and more 'objective' measures of health, such as the EQ-5D health index (described in detail in Chapter 5), also track with socio-economic status, the gaps in the assessments of satisfaction are much smaller than gaps in objective conditions (quality, access, outcomes) would predict.[11] The same often holds across education, job, and economic satisfaction domains, depending on the sample.[12]

Lora and collaborators, and Chattopadhyay and I (using different data sets for Latin America), find that respondents in poor countries are more or

[11] The EQ-5D is a five-part question developed for the British general population, and now widely used in other contexts. The descriptive dimensions are: mobility, self-care, usual activities, pain/discomfort, and anxiety/depression, with the possible answers for each being: no health problems, moderate health problems, and extreme health problems. See Shaw et al. (2005).

[12] Of course, this could also be considered a pessimism bias of the rich.

at least as likely to be satisfied with their health systems than are respondents in wealthier ones, while respondents in some very poor countries, such as Guatemala, have much higher levels of health satisfaction than do those in much wealthier ones with better health systems, such as Chile. Deaton finds the same pattern—or lack of one—with satisfaction with health systems in the worldwide Gallup Poll. While there are surely outliers, objective health conditions—as measured by indicators, such as morbidity and life expectancy—are materially better in the wealthier countries.[13] Cross-country comparisons of average levels of personal health satisfaction demonstrate a similar, although not as notable, pattern. Health satisfaction seems to be more closely associated with cultural differences across countries than it is with objective indicators, such as life expectancy and infant mortality, or with per capita incomes.

Within countries, wealthier respondents are more likely to be happier and more satisfied with their health than are poor ones. Despite the aggregate pattern, though, there is clearly an 'optimism bias' in the responses of the poorest respondents across many domains—health as well as many others, at least in Latin America. For example, those in the highest quintile in the region hold 57% of the income (on average), while those in the poorest quintile hold 4%. But the differences in their perceptions are much smaller. Seventy-nine percent of individuals in the highest quintile declare themselves satisfied with their material or economic quality of life, while 57% of those in the lowest quintile say they are satisfied.[14] There is a similar 'optimism bias' in the responses of the poor as they assess their living conditions and public policies in their countries. The gaps in the

[13] Deaton (2008); Graham and Chattopadhyay (2009); IADB (2008).
[14] Graham and Lora (forthcoming).

assessments of satisfaction with health, education, and jobs between the rich and the poor are much smaller than the gaps in objective conditions.

This paradox is likely due to lower expectations and available information among those living in poorer contexts, as well as to lower expectations. For wealthier individuals and respondents in wealthier countries, aspirations and awareness of those in wealthier countries may go up as much as, if not more rapidly than, improvements in service provision (and/or economic growth). At the same time, there is also inconsistent usage of available information—such as test scores—among slightly wealthier respondents. A surprisingly small amount of school choice, for example, is informed by test score results.[15] This, among other things, may contribute to increased public frustration in the face of improvements in service quality.

The gaps caused by aspirations bias are greater for personal and more subjective things like personal health status than they are for education. In the case of education, there is usually more objective information available to make assessments, and parents are likely evaluating the education that their children are receiving rather than their own. In the case of financial satisfaction, income levels provide a benchmark for making such assessments, in contrast to personal health status and satisfaction, which lack an analogous general indicator, other than mortality rates, which are an ex post measure, at least for the average individual.

The gaps between perceptions and objective measures seem to be greater at the individual level rather than at the average country level (perhaps not a surprise as there is more variance at the individual level); for richer rather than poorer countries (as relative deprivation effects seem to increase as average wealth increases); and for poorer rather than richer individuals

---

[15] See the chapter on education (Cardenas et al., forthcoming).

(perhaps because they have less good information to make assessments, as well as lower expectations).[16] These gaps between subjective and objective measures across various domains may be part of the explanation for the divergent conclusions over the income happiness relationship and, like that relationship, also vary according to which questions are used and the nature of the objective indicators.

Relative Incomes and Inequality—Part of the Paradox?

Happiness may not be *all* relative, but relative differences do seem to matter. While wealthier people are happier than less wealthy ones on average, people of similar income levels are less happy when the incomes of those in a relevant reference group, ranging from neighbors to professional cohorts, to towns and cities, are higher.[17] These concerns for relative income differences, which in theory are greater as average income levels rise, are often cited as part of the explanation for the Easterlin paradox. The intuition is that until basic needs are met, people are not concerned about relative differences, and the relationship between happiness and income resembles a linear one. At higher levels, however, it curves off and resembles a logarithmic function.

At the same time, micro-level empirical work suggests that concerns for relative income differences arise at surprisingly low levels of income. This is apparent, for example, in the lack of correlation between average per capita incomes and happiness among the less developed country sample

---

[16] Graham and Felton (2006a); IADB (2008).

[17] Graham and Felton (2006a); Luttmer (2005) (Luttmer's work is based on US PUMAs, geographic units which are established in census data, which proxy for neighborhoods); and Kingdon and Knight (2007).

in Pettinato's and my work, as well as in within-country work on Latin America by Andrew Felton and myself, and by Lora and colleagues, as well as on South Africa by Kingdon and Knight.[18] Ravallion and Lokshin test for relative deprivation effects in a much poorer context—Malawi—where basic needs are an issue for the average respondent, and find that they do not matter for most respondents in their sample, but do matter for those who are comparatively better off.[19]

For the Gallup Poll for Latin America, Eduardo Lora and colleagues find that reference group income—defined as similar age, income, and education cohorts—is positively correlated with life satisfaction (the Cantril best possible life question), but negatively correlated with satisfaction with one's standard of living, job, and housing.[20] It is likely that both question framing and variance across domains mediates the extent to which comparison effects matter. Indeed, one hypothesis—which could be tested in future research—is that the frames, which provide more visible or tangible reference points across jobs, housing, and education levels, matter more for comparison effects than they do for absolute ones, while inherent character traits/optimism are more important to open-ended life satisfaction questions. (Alternatively, of course, naturally less happy people might be more likely to be concerned about comparison effects.) In Chapter 5, we show that better reference group health is positive for health satisfaction, controlling for individual levels of health, suggesting that at least in the health domain, signaling effects dominate over comparison effects, most

---

[18] For example, Graham and Felton (2006a) and the research in the IADB (2008) report *Beyond Facts* highlight the extent to which this holds for very poor countries in Latin America; Kingdon and Knight (2007) show that it holds for poor communities in South Africa.

[19] See Ravallion and Lokshin (2005).

[20] IADB (2008).

Table 6.3 Relative incomes and satisfaction domains

The relation between life satisfaction and satisfaction with different domains.

	People with income *above* the regional median	People with income *below* the regional median
Economic satisfaction	0.640***	0.497***
Importance of friends	0.257	0.767***
Work satisfaction	0.269*	0.212
Health satisfaction	0.552	0.094
Housing satisfaction	−0.062	0.199
Liberty satisfaction	−0.027	−0.077
Importance of relegion	0.106	0.106
National economy satisfaction	−0.047	0.103
Trust in medical system	−0.125	−0.006
Satisfied with job market policies	−0.138	−0.056
Trust in education system	−0.270***	−0.175
City satisfaction	0.055	−0.382**
Individual optimism score	0.205***	0.279
Number of observations	2,232	1,485

Notes: * Significant at the 90% level.
** Significant at the 95% level.
*** Significant at the 99% level.
Source: IADB calculations using Gallup (2007).

likely because there are positive externalities related to being surrounded by healthier people.

John Helliwell and colleagues, working with the Gallup Poll (the world sample), find that average per capita income levels are negatively correlated with life satisfaction (again the ladder of life question), controlling for individual levels. The significance goes away when additional questions about basic needs, corruption, and freedom to choose are added to the model specification. When the sample is split according to region, the coefficient on average per capita GDP only remains negative (and significant) for Eastern Europe and the FSU and for Africa, and negative (but not significant) for Latin America. Helliwell posits that, for the sample as a whole, relative income effects are likely mediated by taxes and by the public goods that accompany particular countries' distribution. Concerns for relative differences do not seem to be mediated by public goods in the three regions where the ability of the state to provide public goods has either been dramatically shaken or was very weak to begin with.

In earlier work on Latin America based on the Latinobarometro, Andrew Felton and I find that average country-level incomes do not matter to individual happiness, but relative income differences—measured as distance from the mean for the average income in one's country—do matter. We looked at the effects of relative differences both across countries in the region and across city sizes. The relative income effects hold for both, with the only difference being that when the reference group was cities rather than countries, average wealth mattered (negatively) for happiness in addition to relative distance from the average. With a smaller-scale reference group, it is likely that individuals are more influenced by comparison effects (which they can make more easily at the city than at the country level), see Table 6.4.

Based on the coefficient on relative income on happiness, and a four-point happiness scale, our findings suggest that inequality makes the poor in the region three percentage points less happy, and the wealthy five percentage points happier. The difference between the two groups, meanwhile, is an artifact of construction, as the relative distances of the rich from the mean are typically larger than those of the poor.

Figure 6.2 provides a graphic illustration of the implications of these findings. The figure compares a Chilean and a Honduran who are each in the poorest quintile for their country. Even though the poor Chilean is twice as wealthy as the poor Honduran, his or her distance from Chilean mean income is far greater than that of the poor Honduran from mean

Table 6.4 Average versus relative wealth
Ordered logit estimation of a 1–4 scale of happiness.

	Average wealth calculated by:					
	Country	Country	Country city size	Country city size	Country city size	Country city size
Individual wealth	0.1117583		0.1121746		0.0968018	
	5.44**		−6.9**		7.96**	
Average wealth	−0.0523256	0.0594327	0.0543354	0.0578392	−0.0805081	0.0162937
	−0.70	0.78	−0.92	0.99	−2.19*	0.42
Relative wealth		0.1117583		0.1121746		0.0968018
		5.44**		6.9**		7.96**
Country dummies*	N	N	N	N	Y	Y
Citysml dummies	Y	Y	Y	Y	Y	Y
Cluster by:	country	country	country citysml	country citysml	country citysml	country citysml

Notes: Demographic variables in all regressions: age, age-squared, years education, married, male, health, unemp, self-emp, retired, and student.
When we run split sample regressions, by city size, average wealth is positive and significant for small cities.
* T-statistics underneath coefficients.
** indicates significance at the 5% and 1% levels.

Honduran income. Because average country income levels do not matter to happiness, but relative distances from the average do, the poor Honduran is happier because their distance from mean income is smaller. On the other end of the distribution, a wealthy Honduran in the top quintile is happier than a much wealthier Chilean in their top quintile because the former's distance from mean income is greater (see Figure 6.2).

Our findings depart from those of Alesina, di Tella, and MacCulloch for the United States and Europe, where the effects of inequality (albeit measured very differently) on individual happiness are very modest. The starkest contrast is the United States, where the only group that is made less happy by inequality is left-leaning rich people! In the United States,

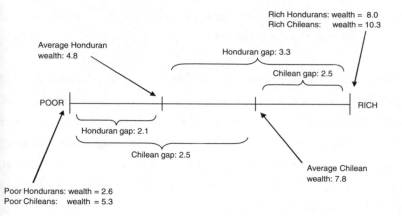

Happiness Gap = wealth gap * coefficient ÷ 4

	Calculated happiness gap	
	Poor	Rich
Chile wealth gap	−2.489	2.521
Honduras wealth gap	−2.142	3.261
Chile-Honduras difference	0.347	0.740
difference * coefficient / 4 = Honduran happiness differential	0.43%	0.93%

	Mean happiness (1–5 scale)			Mean wealth (1–11 scale)		
Wealth quintile	Chile	Honduras	Overall	Chile	Honduras	Overall
1	2.54	3.11	2.73	5.26	2.64	3.12
2	2.74	3.15	2.85	7.00	4.00	5.00
3	2.77	3.17	2.91	8.00	5.00	6.00
4	2.94	3.13	2.97	9.00	6.00	7.46
5	3.08	3.30	3.08	10.27	8.04	9.63
Total	2.79	3.17	2.88	7.76	4.78	5.81

Figure 6.2 A tale of two countries—comparing a rich and a poor person in Honduras and Chile

inequality remains for many respondents a sign of future opportunities and mobility, even though the data on mobility rates no longer support that perception.[21] We posit that in Latin America, in contrast, inequality

---

[21] Alesina et al. (2004); Benabou and Ok (1998); Graham and Young (2003).

is still a sign of persistent advantage for the rich and disadvantage for the poor, even though the data show more mobility than public perceptions suggest.[22]

Country-level aggregations may not be the most relevant ones for studying concerns about relative income differences; the average person may be more concerned with reference groups, such as neighbors or the workplace, where comparisons are more visible. We find that the relative income effect holds and is indeed more notable across cities of different sizes. It is stronger for large cities, where there is more income variance, and smaller for small cities, where average income levels are positively and significantly correlated with happiness, while relative incomes are still negatively correlated with happiness in the small cities.[23] These findings are in keeping with those of Erzo Luttmer for the United States. Luttmer looks across PUMAs in the US census tract and finds that higher average income levels are associated with lower levels of happiness and financial satisfaction, once the effects of individual incomes are controlled for. The effects on financial satisfaction, meanwhile, are much stronger than those for life satisfaction.[24] It may be that PUMAs, like our Latin American cities, provide a smaller reference group frame, in which comparison effects are more likely to be relevant, including in the United States, where the effects of inequality on welfare tend to be more modest.

The relevant reference group likely also varies across cohorts and countries and may then still be subject to change. Pettinato and I find that our frustrated achievers assess their living standards favorably in comparison to

---

[22] See also Graham (2007).

[23] Because there is not a good income variable in the Latinobarometro, the authors use an index of assets to proxy for wealth/income. See Graham and Felton (2006a).

[24] Luttmer (2005).

others in their community, but much more negatively when the reference group is expanded beyond the community to others in their country, a reference group that became more relevant as information and technology, such as the internet, became more widely available. The Kingdon and Knight work on China shows that recent migrants quickly change their reference group to their new urban counterparts rather than the living standards in their towns of origin.

When the Gallup Latin America sample is split into above and below the regional median income groups, the comparison effect holds for both groups, with the difference being that friends satisfaction is significant and positive for the below median group, but insignificant for the rich, while job satisfaction is significant and positive for the rich but not for the poor, implying that the poor and the rich value different domains as they make comparisons, see Table 6.3. When the sample is split into urban and rural, the effects largely hold for the urban cohorts but not for the rural ones (analogous to Felton's and my city size findings).[25]

The evidence suggests that concerns for relative income differences matter and can erode the positive effects of higher absolute income levels on happiness, thus helping to explain the Easterlin paradox. It also suggests that they hold at surprisingly low levels of income, as is suggested by the lack of a clear income–happiness relationship within some less developed country (LDC) samples. Yet it is difficult to be conclusive about how relative differences mediate the Easterlin paradox. One reason for this is that different reference groups matter to different cohorts or cultures, and country-level incomes may not be the most relevant comparator group in many instances. In addition, concerns for relative income differences

[25] IADB (2008).

are mediated by perceptions about what inequality signals, as well as the availability (or not) of public goods.

Much Unhappier than Growth: Financial Crises and Well-Being

Financial crises are terrible for happiness. This is not a surprise. We know that individuals are loss averse and do not like uncertainty. Crises bring about both significant losses and uncertainty. Not surprisingly they bring movements in happiness that are of an unusual magnitude. While national average happiness levels do not move much for the most part, they surely do at times of crisis, although they eventually adapt back.

In a first look at these issues some years ago, Sandip Sukhtankar and I examined the effects of the 2001–2002 crisis in Latin America on happiness. We separated our sample of 18 countries in the Latinobarometro data set into those countries that had experienced negative levels of GDP growth (the crisis countries) and those that had not. While this is far from a perfect definition of crisis, it is surely a parsimonious one.

We found that individuals in the countries that experienced crisis had above average happiness levels before the crisis, and below average levels after (controlling for the usual socio-economic and demographic factors). Yet in the years after the crisis stabilized and growth recovered, average levels in most of the crisis countries recovered to above average levels, see Figure 6.3.

We asked an additional question: did crisis also result in reduced support for democracy and market reforms? These were the two pillars of a decade-long dual transition in the region. Our findings on this front were compelling. We found that while levels of support for the market as a

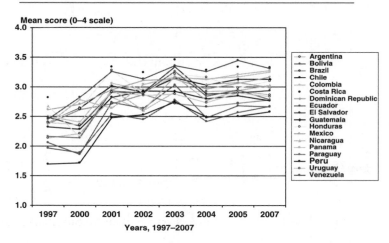

Well-being (happiness): country time trends
Steady since 2001; Costa Rica and Venezuela happiest

Figure 6.3 Happiness in Latin America over time

system and preference for democracy as a system of government were lower than average in the crisis countries before the crisis, they rose to average levels (for market support) and above average levels (for democratic government support) by the end of the crisis. At the same time, satisfaction with how these systems were *performing* went down in the same countries, see Table 6.5. In other words, citizens were able to distinguish between the systems per se, and how particular governments were performing. Citizens seemed to affirm the importance of supporting the systems at a time that economic well-being was increasingly challenged. We found this to be evidence of a significant change in public attitudes in a region with a past trajectory of having citizens calling in the military to intervene at times of crisis.

Table 6.5 Satisfaction with, and support for, market policies and democracy (Latin America 2002)

	Market satisfaction		Support for market		Preference for democracy		Satisfaction with	
	Coefficient	Z stat	Coefficient	Z stat	Coefficient	Z Stat	Coefficient	Z Stat
Age	−0.0098	−8.33	−0.0083	−6.56	0.0204	3.26	0.0069	1.24
Age^2					−0.0002	−2.26	−0.0001	−1.80
Male	0.1110	3.41	0.1001	2.88	0.0358	0.97	0.0617	1.91
Married	−0.0977	−3.08	0.0014	0.04	0.0149	0.41	−0.0646	−1.99
Wealth index	0.0240	3.84	−0.0078	−1.17	0.0260	3.70	−0.0018	−0.30
Education	−0.0557	−14.71	−0.0284	−6.99	0.0211	4.92	−0.0346	−9.19
Employment categories								
Unemployed	−0.1981	−3.2	−0.0431	−0.65	0.0116	0.17	−0.3170	−5.14
Self-employed	−0.0412	−0.89	−0.0127	−0.25	0.0415	0.80	−0.1524	−3.29
Public employee	0.2175	3.54	−0.0058	−0.09	0.0308	0.44	0.0539	0.89
Private employee	0.0275	0.52	−0.0310	−0.54	0.0613	1.04	−0.0477	−0.91
Student	0.0855	1.29	−0.0595	−0.84	0.1434	1.88	−0.0908	−1.36
Retired	0.0021	0.03	0.0609	0.77	0.2639	3.06	0.2936	3.99
Crisis	−0.3391	−11.26	−0.0091	−0.28	0.1963	5.84	−0.2013	−6.73
# of observations	16626		14817		15894		16536	
Pseudo R^2	0.0104		0.003		0.0055		0.005	

Notes: 1. Based on 17 countries.

2. Crisis has a negative but not-significant effect on support for market policies in 2002 but it is significant when data for 2001 and 2000 are considered.

Sources: Author's calculations based on Latinobarometro (2002).

The Mother of All Crises: The 2008–2009 Global Meltdown

Since our initial work on crisis, the 2008 financial market collapse has made the 2001–2002 Latin America down turn, or even the 1998 collapse of the ruble in Russia, pale in terms of magnitude and reach. While I write this at a time when the extent, duration, and magnitude of the crisis is not yet clear, it surely is having and will have effects on the welfare of billions of individuals for the foreseeable future. Those effects are due as much to the welfare losses that have been and will be incurred in incomes and jobs, as to the uncertainty surrounding the crisis and its causes. Economists have been debating the causes, consequences, and possible cures of the crisis for several months since its onset. Our experience with a crisis of this magnitude, and with such strong global inter-connectedness between the markets and countries involved, is limited, with only the Great Depression to point to as an example. Yet that example is one in which global information and technology could not transmit problems—and perhaps solutions—as quickly as they can now.

The crisis has shaken the fundamentals of capitalism, our financial markets are in turmoil, and even the safety of individual bank accounts is in question. The crisis will, no doubt, have profound welfare effects which will be assessed ex post by standard economic analysis of the costs to GNP, savings, investment, and the average consumer. But short of that, how can we assess the impact of the current crisis on individual welfare? Can we estimate the happiness effects of the financial crisis?

It is obviously too soon to do so precisely and impossible to do so at a global level. However, we can get a sense of how financial crises affect national happiness—with a focus here on the United States—based on

169

other countries' recent experiences. During the recent economic crises in Russia and Argentina, for example, happiness levels fell significantly: 8.7% in Russia and 10.7% in Argentina. It is important to put these movements in perspective: average national happiness levels do not move much, if at all, over time. Happiness levels in the United States from the 1970s until the present have not changed much, even though it has been a period of unprecedented prosperity. To the extent they have changed, they have dipped downward very slightly (the explanation usually given for that drop is the unevenly shared nature of the economic gains during that same period).

It is impossible to predict how much the crisis will affect US GDP growth, although it likely will have some negative effect. By early 2009, unemployment rates had already risen by several percentage points. Argentina's GDP fell by ten percentage points in 2002 alone. Such a large drop is unlikely in the United States. Yet the psychological shock effect of major banks and other financial institutions failing in a traditionally stable economy—indeed for years *the* model for capitalism—is likely much higher. Research on other countries suggests that the unhappiness effects of crises are as much due to the uncertainty they generate as they are to the actual drops in income levels that they cause. In order to estimate the possible orders of magnitude, we simulated a happiness drop in the United States that is equivalent to that in Argentina in 2001. Accepting that is an upper limit on what is likely to occur in the United States, we calculated the income equivalent required to compensate for such a loss in reported happiness for the average individual (based on the coefficient on income in the standard happiness regression for the United States, which appears in Table 3.1 in Chapter 3). It would be comparable to a 75% decline in income, or $45,000 for a person

---

Crises and happiness: An illustration

- **Decline in happiness scores with economic crises:**
- Russia, 1998: Decline from 2.3 to 2.1 (1–5 scale)
- Argentina, 2002: Decline from 2.8 to 2.5 (1–4 scale)
- USA, 2008: Assume matching decline 0.225 (1–3 scale)
- **(matching US to ~ 10% decline in Russia and Argentina)**
- **Extrapolating using CSS data for US:**
- Δ happy = 0.163 * Δ ln(income)
- Δ ln(Income) = −0.225/0.163 = − 1.3803
- Assume Y_0 = Median US annual HH income = $60000
- Then Y_1 = $15,100
- Hence an income equivalent of happiness decline of about $44900
- Impact of current crisis on happiness in Russia? Will higher unemployment rate regions suffer less from crisis precisely because they have integrated/reformed less?

Figure 6.4 Crisis and happiness

earning $60,000.[26] And while this estimate is by definition imprecise, it suggests that the well-being losses for the average person associated with the crisis are very large, see Figure 6.4.

---

[26] Argentina's drop of 0.3 on a 1–4 happiness scale is equivalent to a 0.225 drop on the US 1–3 happiness scale in the General Social Survey (pooled data for 1972–1998). The coefficient on log income for the United States is 0.163. Thus the income equivalent of a 0.225 drop in happiness translates into an income change of 1 ÷ 3.97 (roughly one-fourth of the previous level). For more detail on the method, see Graham and Chattopadhyay (2008a).

What are the implications of generalized happiness falls of such magnitude? Much of the research discussed in this book shows that happier people are more likely to support markets and democracy; to perform better in the labor market and to be healthier; and to have positive attitudes about future mobility for themselves and their children. We do not know if short-term but significant happiness drops erode these positive associations over the long term, but they surely could. It will be difficult to measure this accurately until well after the end of the crisis.

Related to this, the strong belief in opportunity and upward mobility is the explanation that is often given for Americans' high tolerance for inequality: the majority of Americans surveyed believe that they will be above mean income in the future (even though that is a mathematical impossibility).[27] Will the crisis erode the longstanding belief in America as the land of opportunity?

Happiness levels typically recover along with economies. Argentines and Russians have by now reached their pre-crisis happiness levels. In Argentina, levels of satisfaction with markets and democracy, and prospects for upward mobility, have also recovered somewhat, although they still remain well below the average for Latin America. To the extent that happiness levels drop in the United States, they will also likely recover over time, although the estimates above suggest that significant welfare losses could be incurred in the process. An open question is whether those losses will erode faith in the fairness of the economic system—both within and outside the United States—not least because the costs of the crisis will be paid for by the average citizen, while its roots lie in weak regulation and excessively compensated executive mismanagement.

[27] See Graham and Young (2003).

To the extent that we have past experience, our research on Latin America suggests that at times of crisis citizens are able to distinguish between the poor performance and mistakes of particular governments and the more general economic and governance systems they live under. Hopefully the well-being losses associated with this crisis will similarly result in positive momentum for necessary adjustments to national and international systems of economy and governance rather than a dramatic refutation of those systems. While it is too early to answer this question—or to accurately gauge the well-being costs of the crisis—we can surely posit that those costs are high, and they make whatever unhappiness is caused by rapid economic growth pale in comparison.

The Misery Index: Inflation versus Unemployment

The misery index is a well-known concept in standard economics textbooks and literature. It is a concept which attempts to gauge the negative effects that both inflation and unemployment have on welfare, and is used as a way to measure the effects of each of these two phenomena on a particular country's citizens' welfare, depending on what the respective rates may be at any point in time. The misery index assumes a straightforward one to one trade-off for inflation versus unemployment. In other words, raising the inflation rate 1% has equivalent negative effects on welfare, as does raising the unemployment rate. While there is nothing necessarily wrong with this assumption, research based on happiness surveys suggests that the trade-off may be quite different for most individuals.

Happiness research highlights the deleterious effects of unemployment on welfare, thus suggesting that the unemployment rate may have stronger welfare effects than the inflation rate, for a number of reasons. First of all, unemployment is one of the variables—along with ill health—that has one of the most consistent and strong effects on well-being. Second, the few studies that have been done comparing the effects of the two on individual welfare suggest that the effects of higher unemployment rates on happiness are an order of magnitude greater than those of inflation.[28] Third, most of what we know from the happiness literature and research supports this. While higher inflation rates may erode purchasing power, they may also be associated with things that raise happiness in the short term, such as lower taxes and other expenditure burdens. To the extent individuals are hyperbolic discounters, most would opt for higher levels of inflation before they accepted the typical fiscal tightening (and consumption loss-related) measures that would be necessary to reduce inflation. Unemployment, meanwhile, is usually associated with losses of both income and status, both of which have been shown to have extremely negative effects on welfare.

Di Tella, MacCulloch, and Oswald, for example, find that unemployment has far greater costs for happiness in the OECD countries than does inflation—at a ratio of about four to one—certainly much higher than the standard misery index. More recent work by Paul Luengas and Inder Ruprah, meanwhile, finds that the cost of inflation in terms of unemployment is about one to eight for Latin America—almost double what has been found for OECD countries. The latter also find that the costs of unemployment are higher for the young and for left-leaning citizens.[29]

While one would not want to calculate a new misery index based on the results of happiness surveys, not least due to the inter-temporal problems discussed above, policy design could surely be informed by what happiness

---

[28] See Clark and Oswald (1994); Di Tella et al. (2001); Graham and Pettinato (2002a); Luengas and Ruprah (2008).

[29] Di Tella et al. (2001); Luengas and Ruprah (2008).

surveys tell us about these trade-offs. The much higher value that most of the world's citizens place on unemployment versus inflation suggests that its solution should be strongly on the policy agenda. Inflation, meanwhile, has usually been studied when it is at moderate or moderately high levels. This is not the case of hyperinflations, which erode both purchasing power and faith in public institutions, ranging from the government, to the currency, to law enforcement officials. While we do not have data available, a study of the difference between the welfare effects of hyperinflations versus those of more moderate levels could inform future discussions of the appropriate calculation of the misery index.

Unemployment

One of the most important variables affecting well-being or happiness is employment status. Previous happiness research has found that unemployment is one of the most traumatic events that can happen to people. One of the reasons for this is of course the loss of income; however, there is also a cultural stigma to unemployment that impacts happiness.

The strength of these effects—for example, the 'costs' of unemployment—tend to vary across countries and regions. We build on the work of others. Di Tella, MacCulloch, and Oswald find that respondents in the United States and Europe are made more unhappy by higher unemployment rates than they are by inflation.[30] In other words, the typical respondent—including employed respondents—would accept higher levels of inflation if it would eliminate the insecurity associated with higher unemployment rates. Several studies have shown that increased unemployment in general lessens the impact on unemployed individuals.

[30] Di Tella et al. (2001).

Clark and Oswald find that the unemployed in the United Kingdom are less unhappy in districts where the unemployment rate is higher.[31] The costs to happiness that come from the decreased probability of finding a job seem to be lower than the gains to happiness that come from being less stigmatized and accompanied by more unemployed counterparts. Similarly, Stutzer and Lalive find that unemployed respondents are less happy in cantons that have voted to reduce unemployment benefits in Switzerland (controlling for benefit levels), as the stigma from unemployment is higher.

In a departure from most of the literature on unemployment and happiness, meanwhile, Andrew Eggers, Clifford Gaddy, and I find that *both* employed and unemployed respondents are happier in regions with higher unemployment rates in Russia, based on the Russian Longitudinal Monitoring Survey (RLMS).[32] While the effects of higher rates on the unemployed are expected, those on the employed are not. Employed people are usually made unhappy by higher unemployment rates, whether it is because they see a higher probability of becoming unemployed themselves, or because they fear the negative externalities—such as higher rates of crime or tax burdens—that typically accompany unemployment rates. The findings for Russia are indeed distinct. Russians are surely made less happy by higher national unemployment rates (which we control for in our regressions); however, the variance among regional rates clearly shows higher happiness levels in higher unemployment rate regions among both employed and unemployed respondents, see Table 6.6.

These findings might be a reflection of some odd Russian *schadenfreude*—'I feel better off if those around me are worse off'—which could be

---

[31] Clark and Oswald (1994).
[32] Eggers et al. (2006); Stutzer and Lalive (2004).

Table 6.6 Happiness and regional unemployment rates in Russia

Ordered logit regression; dependent variable reported life satisfaction (1, 2, 3, 4, 5)	Complete regression results						
	Marginal effect: change in probability of scoring 1 out of 5 in life satisfaction[1]	Coefficient estimate	SEs corrected for auto-correlation w/i individuals		SEs corrected for correlation of residuals w/i regions		
			Signif[2]	z		Signif	z
Lagged satisfaction	−0.115	0.600	***	41.18		***	25.95
Age	0.170	−0.047	***	−10.08		***	−7.48
Age²	−0.138	0.000	***	8.65		***	7.21
Male	−0.030	0.172	***	6.86		***	6.75
Real household equivalence income[3]	−0.023	0.260	***	6.9		***	3.27
Regional unemployment rate	0.026	4.239	***	4.88		**	2.25
Income quartile within region[4]							
Second quartile	−0.010	0.058	*	1.76			1.41
Third quartile	−0.045	0.263	***	7.67		***	5.36
Fourth quartile	−0.078	0.470	***	11.1		***	5.81
Educational attainment[5]							
Finished high school	0.011	−0.060	*	−1.7			−1.58
Attended some university	−0.014	0.080	**	2.43		**	2.49
Marriage status[6]							
Married	−0.010	0.055		1.54			1.21
Divorced	0.024	−0.130	**	−2.42		**	−2.37
Widowed	0.010	−0.055		−0.96			−0.79

(cont.)

Table 6.6 (*Continued*)

Ordered logit regression; dependent variable reported life satisfaction (1, 2, 3, 4, 5)[7]	Complete regression results					
	Marginal effect: change in probability of scoring 1 out of 5 in life satisfaction[1]	Coefficient estimate	SEs corrected for auto-correlation w/i individuals		SEs corrected for correlation of residuals w/i regions	
			Signif[2]	z	Signif	z
Employment categories[7]						
Self-employed	−0.073	0.474	***	4.94	***	3.9
Retired	0.035	−0.193	***	−4.4	***	−5.04
Student	−0.026	0.152	**	2.59	**	2.44
Housewife	−0.028	0.165	***	2.91	***	3.31
Unemployed	0.108	−0.547	***	−12.02	***	−9.3
Round dummies[8]						
Round 7 (Oct–Dec 1996)	−0.053	0.314	***	6.25	***	3.58
Round 8 (Oct 1998–Jan 1999)		dropped				
Round 9 (Sept–Dec 2000)	−0.127	0.809	***	17.85	***	12.91
Round 10 (Sept–Dec 2001)	−0.160	1.035	***	19.87	***	11.58
Regional dummies		38 included				
Cut points			Standard errors of cut points			
_cut1		0.268	0.184		0.372	
_cut2		2.130	0.185		0.339	
_cut3		3.474	0.186		0.344	
_cut4		5.412	0.189		0.357	

Regression statistics

Number of observations	27517	27517
Wald chi2(58)	5689.1	.9
Prob > chi2	0	.9
Pseudo R^2	0.0928	0.0928
Log likelihood	−35429.2	−35429.2

Notes: [1] Marginal effects reflect the change in the probability of scoring 'Not at all satisfied' on the RLMS with a given change in the independent variable—a one standard deviation change in the continuous variables and a change from 0 to 1 in the dummy variables.

[2] * Indicates significant at 10%; ** at 5%; and *** at 1%.

[3] The RLMS asks each individual to report his or her income for the previous month. We created a measure of household equivalence income by summing the income reported by all members of a single household in the RLMS survey (which measures income in the past month) and dividing it by the square root of the number of people in that household. To convert this value into a real figure, we used a CPI measure from the International Monetary Fund's *International Financial Statistics*. The calculation was complicated by the fact that Russia dropped three zeros from the ruble denomination on January 1, 1998. To improve the comparability of scale in the coefficients, we multiplied the coefficient on real household euqivalence income by 1,000 on this table.

[4] Omitted group is the lowest income quartile. We calculate the income quartiles region by region using household equivalence income.

[5] Omitted group did not finish high school.

[6] Omitted group is single.

[7] Omitted group is employed outside of the home.

[8] The regression makes use of lagged satisfaction responses from Round 6, October–December 1995. Since lagged responses were missing for every respondent in Round 6, the regression makes use of responses from rounds 7–10 and drops a round for multicollinearity.

[9] It is not possible to calculate these statistics when errors are assumed to be correlated with a variable that is in the model (in this case, region dummies).

understandable in the context of dramatic reform and high levels of macroeconomic volatility, as in Russia from 1995 to 2000. We attribute our findings to a related trend—a fear of reform or uncertainty trend. The regions with higher unemployment rates are also those that have, for the most part, undertaken far less extensive reforms than those such as Moscow or St Petersburg. Thus citizens are typically living in a low-level economic equilibrium, with little market activity (and some even operating on a barter basis) and some form of pre-existing industry-based safety nets, and with relatively low levels of inequality. Most individuals are risk averse, and those in regions with more reforms have had to deal with much more uncertainty related to change, as well as with increasing differences between those that benefit from reforms and those that do not.

Supporting this 'fear of change or reform' interpretation, we find that it is those respondents with the most precarious, low-level jobs that are made most 'happy' by higher unemployment rates. They are also the cohorts that most quickly would lose their jobs were extensive reforms put in place. We view these findings as much as an insight into the particulars of the Russian context as into the ways in which unemployment can affect well-being.

In Latin America, based on the Latinobarometro survey, Stefano Pettinato and I also find positive effects of general unemployment on happiness, using both an unemployment rate calculated from our own data and the latest statistics available from the United Nations Economic Commission for Latin America and the Caribbean (ECLAC). These are country-wide unemployment rates and have statistically significant positive effects on happiness. As in the above studies, higher overall unemployment may reduce the stigma effect on individuals. The results must be tempered, though, by the limited information that open unemployment rates can provide in a region with high levels of informal employment (exceeding 50% in a few countries).

Based on later years of the same survey, Andrew Felton and I looked more closely at the happiness effects of unemployment in Latin America, both across countries and across cities of different sizes within them. Small cities were those with less than 5,000 people; medium-sized cities ranged from above 5,000 to 100,000 inhabitants; and large cities were those with over 100,000 inhabitants. The typical unemployed person in our study is a male who has attended some high school (on average ten years of education). The unemployed percentage of the population increases with city size. This may be an artifact of the data, however, because people in rural areas are more likely to be outside the formal labor force altogether and unemployment is a less relevant concept for them.

Inequality in countries also has an effect on happiness among the unemployed. Using our pooled data set from 1997–2004, we ran a standard happiness regression, including a control variable for being unemployed, and then adding interaction terms for being unemployed in a high or low Gini country. We find that the costs to happiness of being unemployed are lower in higher Gini countries. In other words, unemployed respondents in countries with higher inequality are actually happier than those in countries with low inequality. Countries with high inequality are also, on balance, poorer than other countries, so the unemployed may have less far to fall, see Table 6.7a.

Another reason may be the higher levels of informal employment in the poorer and more unequal countries in the region, thereby resulting in less stigma for the unemployed. Or it may be due to some other country-level unobservable that we are not accounting for. And while the costs of being unemployed are *lower* in higher Gini countries, fear of unemployment

181

Table 6.7a Cost of unemployment

	Coefficient	z-score
Ordered logit regression of a 1–5 scale of happiness for 2004 data set. Controls include standard demographic variables and country dummies.		
Unemployed	−0.342	−6.05**
Ordered logit regression of a 1–5 scale of happiness for pooled 1997–2004 data set. Controls include standard demographic variables, country dummies and year dummies.		
Unemployed	−1.375	−5.07**
Unemployed*gini coefficient	0.020	3.93**
Ordered logit regression of a 1–5 scale of happiness. Controls include standard demographic variables and country dummies. Costs of unemployment by education level. Base case is illiterate.		
Unemployed (incomplete primary)	−0.485	−3.83**
Unemployed (completed primary)	−0.205	−1.63
Unemployed (incomplete secondary)	−0.511	−4.46**
Unemployed (completed secondary)	−0.562	−5.17**
Unemployed (incomplete tertiary)	0.027	0.13
Unemployed (completed tertiary)	−0.246	−1.39

(among the employed) is *higher*, in keeping with our intuition about greater levels of informality and associated insecurity. Thus in higher inequality countries, the lower stigma for the unemployed is accompanied by greater insecurity for the employed.

Job instability has particularly affected those with a high school level of education, and if we look at the happiness impact of unemployment among different educational groups, it turns out that, in addition to having the highest rate of unemployment, those with a high school education are also made most unhappy by unemployment. In fact, unemployment has a statistically insignificant effect on happiness at the ends of the education spectrum. College-educated people are also less likely to fear unemployment than those with less education. And unemployment is a less relevant concept

Table 6.7b Fear of unemployment

	Coefficient	z-score
Ordered logit regression of a 1–5 scale of fear of unemployment. Controls include standard demographic variables (except dummy variables for jobs that. are not in the workforce) and country dummies.		
Small town	−0.256	−4.34[**]
Big city	0.081	1.87
Ordered logit regression of a 1–5 scale of fear of unemployment Controls include standard demographic variables (except dummy variables for jobs that are not in the workforce)		
Gini coefficient	0.017	4.45[**]

for the illiterate, who are most likely to be outside the formal labor market to begin with, and those with higher education are more likely to be able to find another job than those with secondary school education, see Table 6.7a.

We also looked at the costs to unemployment by city size. As in the case of our Gini coefficients, we find that the costs of unemployment are lower in big cities than they are in small towns, suggesting that there is a lower stigma effect in big cities. Yet again, as in the case of inequality (as measured by the Gini), fear of unemployment is higher in the big cities, presumably because labor markets are more integrated into the international economy and volatility is more of a factor, while relying on farming as a safety net is not an option the way it is in smaller towns (see Table 6.7b).

Our findings are suggestive of how the costs of being unemployed can vary across countries and according to different measures of inequality. Inequality seems to be correlated with a lower 'stigma' for the unemployed, but with a higher fear of unemployment for the employed. Unemployment, meanwhile, affects people via income and non-income channels. Surely the loss of income has a role. Yet the findings on stigma suggest that the non-income channels are also quite important. While being unemployed is a bad thing for happiness regardless of the context, it is much less bad in those contexts where there are more unemployed companions around, even though that in and of itself suggests that the probability of becoming re-employed—and earning more income in the future—is much lower. In Chapter 7, we show how similar channels affect the relationship between crime victimization and well-being. Both sets of findings are examples of how other factors mediate the income-happiness relationship and at times in unexpected ways.

Conclusions

The discussion in this chapter highlights the complexity of the relationship between happiness and income, and how it is mediated by a range of other factors, such as health, which was discussed in Chapter 5, and institutional regimes, which are discussed in Chapter 7. The complexity seems to increase as countries go up the development ladder. As levels go up, rising aspirations and increasing awareness interact with pre-existing cultural and normative differences, as well as both the extent and quality of public goods, which are in part endogenous to these cultural and normative differences. At the same time, because global information and access to a range of technologies are now available to countries at much lower levels of per capita incomes, benefits associated with higher incomes, such as better health care, are often available in contexts with much lower levels of per capita incomes than was previously possible. Not surprisingly, all of these factors—and how they are or are not captured in the survey data that are used—come into play in the debate over how much happiness levels increase as countries grow wealthier.

The chapter also demonstrates that the *processes* related to generating income, such as economic growth and its fluctuations, as well as the supporting institutional arrangements, such as market regimes and the nature of governments, also have effects on well-being, and sometimes unexpected ones. While sharp drops in growth and related increases in insecurity at times of crisis are surely bad for well-being, rapid periods of growth also have surprising negative effects, effects which are likely related to concerns about inequality and changing rewards to different skill sets, among other things.

Changes in employment status that result from economic cycles and structural changes also affect well-being, but again in unpredictable ways. While unemployment, for example, is a bad thing, it seems to be worse in contexts where people are less accustomed to it. Inequality, meanwhile, is good or bad for well-being, depending on what it signals. In the United States, where it is still seen as a sign of opportunity, it does not seem to have consistent effects on well-being. In Latin America, in contrast, where inequality is still seen as a sign of persistent advantage for the rich and disadvantage for the poor, the aggregate welfare effects of inequality are negative (as there are many more poor than there are rich in the region).

Given the range of factors and the often competing channels through which they affect well-being, it is, perhaps, not a great surprise that the relationship between income and happiness across countries is the subject of continued debate, above and beyond the methodological issues and questions that were raised in the previous chapter. And while some of the results based on happiness surveys—such as the paradox of unhappy growth and the preference that the unemployed have for higher levels of unemployment—do not translate easily or directly into policy terms, they provide insights into how the processes of development and income generation affect individual well-being, and why, at times, there is a remarkable amount of public frustration when times are 'good' by standard definition, as well as complacency when times are 'bad'.

CHAPTER 7

Adapting to Good and Bad Fortune

How Friends, Freedom, Crime, and Corruption affect Happiness

A lawyer with his briefcase can steal more than a hundred men with guns. **Don Corleone,** *The Godfather*

When I sell liquor, it's called bootlegging; when my patrons serve it on Lake Shore Drive, it's called hospitality. **Al Capone**

In the previous chapter, we examined the effects of macroeconomic and related trends on happiness. We have also seen that rapid economic growth can be destabilizing and cause unhappiness, and that people adapt very quickly to whatever economic gains growth brings about. We know that education and having a job make you happier, and that how wealthy you are in relation to other people can affect how happy you are. But what about other factors that affect your day-to-day experience, such as religion, friendships and social networks, personal liberty, participating in politics, and the effects of criminal violence? What kinds of effects do these things have on happiness?

These effects are not always easy to disentangle. Do happier people benefit from democracy or does democracy 'cause' happiness? Does crime cause unhappiness or are unhappy people more likely to report crime and corruption? How do these complex relationships, which have aggregate country-level patterns, affect the income–happiness relationship?

One can imagine average happiness levels being pulled down in a relatively wealthy country which has high levels of crime. Or, in contrast, happiness being higher than predicted by per capita income levels in a poor country with very strong social capital. And it is not clear that crime rates or social capital have the same effects on well-being in every context. An important part of the story is the extent to which people adapt to both good and bad equilibrium, and how that adaptation mediates the effects of contextual factors on well-being. All of these factors, in turn, affect how particular countries fit into the overall income–happiness cross-country scatter plot and help explain why there are so many outliers on that plot.

In the previous chapter we focused on the way in which macroeconomic and related institutional factors affected happiness. In this chapter we focus on public institutions, public goods, and related issues of social capital and social networks. A theme which runs throughout the chapter—and is supported by our empirical findings—is adaptation: expectations rise along with good equilibriums—like high levels of freedom—and then the positive externalities of good equilibrium increase in their importance for happiness as individuals come to expect them. Expectations also decline as individuals adapt to bad equilibrium—like high levels of crime—and then, in turn, the negative externalities from bad equilibrium become less important to happiness.

It is difficult to judge whether rising expectations or downward adaptations are good or bad things; they are likely a part of human nature. Downward adaptation is likely an important survival mechanism at times of adversity. Rising expectations—and resulting demands for higher standards—may have provided impetus to the remarkable progress that humanity has made over time in areas such as technology and health. At the least, better understanding of these traits—and their interaction with the effects of particular institutional arrangements on well-being—may enhance our chances of crafting better policies that can help societies 'tip' from bad to good equilibrium, as in the case of crime and corruption norms.

Social Capital and Friendships

There is a wide literature—pioneered by Robert Putnam—on the importance of social capital to a host of outcomes ranging from economic development to democratic government to health. A review of that literature is surely beyond the scope of this book. Suffice it to note that there is a wide body of empirical evidence linking higher levels of social capital to outcomes that are, on balance, positive for quality of life and economic progress, such as economic growth, better governance, and higher levels of productivity.[1] Given the focus of this book, it raises the obvious question of the linkages between social capital and well-being. Not surprisingly, there are positive links between well-being and friendships, narrowly defined, and social capital, more broadly defined. What is harder to disentangle, though, is whether happier people make more friends and/or interact with others more, or whether friendships and social interactions make people happier. Causality likely runs in both directions, and there is some evidence that there are additional positive externalities from these social dynamics.

---

[1] For a comprehensive review, including of Putnam's work, see Grootaert and van Bastelaer (2002).

In an extensive look at quality of life in Latin America with Eduardo Lora and colleagues, we looked at the importance of friendships. The Gallup World Poll has a variable which asks the respondent whether or not they have friends or relatives they can count on.[2] It turns out that friendships and relatives matter more to the well-being of the average Latin American respondent than health, employment, or personal assets, and only slightly less than food security (of course it could be that happier people are more likely to have and value friendships), see Figure 7.1. This varies according to income levels, with the rich valuing work and health more, and the poor valuing friendships. These friendships most likely provide important coping mechanisms for the poor in the absence of publicly provided safety nets. Whether they serve as strong or weak ties in the Granovetter sense is an open question. Granovetter's work on US workers showed that their 'weak' ties, or their connections beyond their immediate family and friends, were more important to upward mobility than were the 'strong' ties of family and friendship.[3] The life domains that are most relevant to happiness in Latin America are economic satisfaction, the importance of friends, and work, health, and housing satisfaction (in that order of importance).

Reporting religion to be important and having access to a telephone, meanwhile, are also positively correlated with happiness in Latin America. A number of studies show that those who have religious faith are, on average, happier than others. It is not clear whether happier people are more likely to have faith, or whether having religion makes them happy, or if there is a more generalized effect that comes from the social networks that often accompany religiosity. Meanwhile, there has been a proliferation of

---

[2] The question in the Gallup Poll is phrased thus: 'if you were in trouble, do you have friends or relatives you can count on, or not?'

[3] Granovetter (1973).

cell phones in Latin America in recent years, as a result of the privatization of telecommunications. Cell phones are a status good and provide important linkages with job and other networks which large numbers of poor in remote urban shantytowns previously lacked.[4]

John Helliwell has done extensive research into whether living in contexts with greater social capital and with greater freedom play a role in individual well-being. The basic answer is a resounding yes on both fronts. In his most recent paper, based on the Gallup World Poll, Helliwell and colleagues compare the various determinants of well-being across 120 countries in the five regions covered by the Poll.[5] They find that all measures of social connections are significantly correlated with life satisfaction, across the countries and regions in the sample. Respondents seem to value both the support that they get from others and the support that they give to others.

Andrew Clark and Orsolya Lelkes explore the issue of religion in greater detail, and attempt to tease out the differences between belonging to a religion and having faith, on the one hand, and the positive externalities that come from the related social networks, on the other. They look at 90,000 individuals across 26 European countries and find that, not surprisingly, reporting to belong to a religion is positively correlated with life satisfaction. More surprising, though, they find that average religiosity in the region also has a positive impact: people are more satisfied in more religious regions, regardless of whether they themselves are religious or non-believers ('atheists'). The equally surprising flipside is that having a higher proportion

---

[4] Labonne and Chase (2008).

[5] They drop roughly eight countries which do not have specifications for income. See Helliwell et al. (2008). For more detail on the relationship between social capital and trust, and how it varies across cohorts and ethnic boundaries, see Soroka et al. (2007).

of atheists has a negative spillover effect for the religious and for atheists alike.[6]

They find that Catholics and Protestants are each more likely to live in regions where their own religions dominate, but that Protestants are happier than are Catholics when they live in a region where their own religion does not dominate. Their findings on religion, meanwhile, are not explained by general levels of social capital, crime, or trust. It is important to note, though, that their study took place in contexts of moderate rather than extreme religiosity, and that they might be quite different in contexts of extremes, where there was more competition or even animosity among the religions.

In addition to the findings on social capital, there is some evidence from happiness surveys that better health and higher levels of health satisfaction may be connected via social networks or friendships. Eduardo Lora, Lucas Higuera, and I, using Gallup World Poll data and various indicators of health status for Latin America, find that being in a reference group with better than average health status (discussed in detail in Chapter 5) is associated with higher levels of health satisfaction. This effect is independent of the influence of each individual's health status, which we control for. In contrast to reference group income, which tends to be negative for life satisfaction, controlling for own income, due to greed and envy effects, reference group health seems to operate through more positive channels. Being around healthier people likely has positive externalities. In addition, the EQ-5D assessment highlights the role of pain and anxiety in addition to physical health, and one can also imagine that being around anxious people in particular could have negative externalities. Nicholas

---

[6] Clark and Lelkes (2009).

Cristakis and colleagues, using the Framington Heart Study for the United States, find that social influence plays a stronger role in determining health outcomes than do social comparison or relative deprivation effects.[7] The relationship between friendships and well-being seems to cross the bounds between psychological and physical well-being.

A full discussion of why these variables matter is beyond the scope of this book. Yet it is likely that their relative importance varies significantly across countries and cultures, as well as socio-economic levels. Because they mediate the income–happiness relationship, they likely play some role in explaining cross-country discrepancies or anomalies.

Political Freedom, Political Participation, and Happiness

There is substantial work on the effects of political participation—and the nature of government regimes—on happiness. The channels through which these factors operate, however, are not completely clear. One can imagine that the nature of political regimes matters to people's well-being, and that living with freedom and good government is better than not. In his worldwide Gallup Poll study, Helliwell finds that citizens that live in a context of freedom are significantly happier than those that do not. And, as is suggested above, freedom seems to matter more to the happiness of those that have come to expect it than to those that do not. Veenhoven also finds that living in a context of freedom is linked to higher levels of well-being. One issue is that it is difficult to disentangle freedom from other contextual factors, such as the nature of public goods, and other unobservable factors.[8]

---

[7] See DeWan and Christakis (2009); Graham et al. (2009).

[8] Hudson (2006); Veenhoven (2002).

Other studies find that trust in political institutions matters to well-being. Hudson finds that trust in both political institutions—such as the European Union, the United Nations, and one's national government—is closely correlated with happiness. Other studies—including our own—find that having trust in others in general is linked to higher levels of well-being. Of course, the usual problem of not being able to disentangle whether happier people are more likely to have trust, or whether trusting others per se generates happiness, applies. In addition, this relationship between trust and higher levels of well-being is likely stronger in contexts where trusting public institutions is the norm rather than an aberration.

One study, by Bruno Frey and Alois Stutzer, at least partially gets around this problem. They find that, in addition to living with more freedom or in a democratic context, individuals seem to benefit from *participating* in democracy. They distinguish the concept of procedural utility as it applies to political participation. Procedural utility is the utility which comes from participating as distinct from the utility that is the outcome or result of participating. They have a unique data set—based on variance in voting structures across Swiss cantons—in which they test whether voters gain procedural utility from participating in direct democracy. Only nationals are allowed to vote in referendums in Switzerland, but both foreigners and nationals benefit from the outcomes of those votes, and the welfare effects of the latter can also be tested across cantons.

Frey and Stutzer find that there is an additional positive effect on happiness that comes from participating in direct democracy, an effect that is above and beyond that of individual traits, being a national or a foreigner, and the variance in the level of public goods across cantons. Citizens—both nationals and foreigners—that live in jurisdictions with more developed political participation rights have higher happiness levels. However, the positive effect is greater for nationals, reflecting the additional effect that comes from participating in the elections as well as benefiting from them.[9]

Happiness and Democracy in the Developing World

Our own work on the developing and transition economies corroborates the above findings, although it does not solve the direction of causality problem. Stefano Pettinato and I, using Latinobarometro data, found that individual respondents' attitudes about the market and about democracy were positively correlated with happiness. In other words, controlling for other variables such as income and age and using country dummies, individuals with pro-market attitudes were, on average, happier than those who did not favor market policies. Not surprisingly, wealth levels and education levels had positive and significant effects on pro-market attitudes, see Table 7.1. When we look at the inverse relationship, we also find that happier people are more likely to be pro-market, so we have the usual problem of establishing the direction of causality. It may well be that happier individuals are more likely to cast whatever policy environment they inhabit in a favorable light, see Table 7.2.

We also looked at two questions pertaining to democracy. One asked respondents whether democracy was preferable to any other form of government. The other inquired about the respondent's degree of satisfaction with democracy, with four possible answers: not at all satisfied, not very satisfied, satisfied, and very satisfied. When we examined the effects of these two variables on happiness, controlling for the usual demographic

[9] Frey (2008); Frey and Stutzer (2002a).

Table 7.1 Correlates of pro-market attitudes

Latin America, 2000

Dependent variable: pro-market attitudes index	*Coeff.*	*t-stat*
age	−0.003	−3.459
age^2/100	0.003	3.185
male	0.017	3.260
log(wealth)	0.055	9.476
education	0.002	2.226
married	−0.004	−0.745
Employment Status*		
self-employed	0.001	0.137
public employee	−0.009	−0.861
private employee	0.000	0.044
unemployed	−0.021	−1.894
retired	−0.003	−0.205
student	−0.030	−2.938
Intercept	0.575	24.207
R^2	0.014	
Number of obs.	11,928	

Notes: Country fixed-effects estimation
*Omitted reference category is housewives or house/husbands
Source: Authors' calculations from Latinobarometro.

variables and including country dummies, we found that satisfaction with democracy was correlated with higher levels of happiness, while a preference for democracy over other forms of government had no significance. When we included pro-market attitudes in the regression, the effects of satisfaction with democracy remained positive and significant.

These findings are in keeping with those of Ronald Inglehart, who uses data on life satisfaction and political satisfaction from the Eurobarometro survey for nine European nations from 1973 to 1986 (totaling more than 200,000 interviews in more than 200 nationally representative surveys). Inglehart finds that, at the aggregate country level, both political satisfaction and life satisfaction are correlated with stable democracy. The effects of life

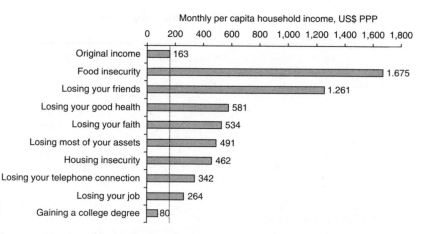

Figure 7.1 Value of food security, friends, and other variables

Notes: Monetary valuation of some life satisfaction determinants (if someone suffers a change in his or her life conditions, what is the new income required to compensate for the related effects?).

Source: *Beyond Facts: Understanding Quality of Life* (Washington DC: Inter-American Development Bank 2008). *IDB calculation using Gallup (2007). The person for this example is a single 30-year-old woman, with no children, a high school degree, employed, with friends and religious beliefs.*

satisfaction are stronger, however, because life satisfaction trends within developed countries are fairly stable over time and seem to be correlated with other traits, such as interpersonal trust. In contrast, political satisfaction fluctuates more, because it behaves like an indicator of public attitudes about government popularity, changing from one month to the next in response to current economic and political events. Political satisfaction levels are only weakly linked with the number of years that democratic institutions have been in place in a given nation (Inglehart's measure of stable democracy), while the link between life satisfaction and stable democracy is higher.[10]

---

[10] The R^2 for correlation between duration of democratic institutions and satisfaction is 0.21, while for the links between life satisfaction and democracy it is 0.85. Inglehart (1988).

Table 7.2 Happiness, market, and democracy preferences
Latin America, 2000

Dependent variable: happiness	(1)		(2)	
	Coeff.	*z-stat*	*Coeff.*	*z-stat*
Age	−0.014	−1.99	−0.008	−1.24
Age^2/100	0.011	1.46	0.001	0.13
Male	0.050	1.29	0.036	0.92
log(wealth)	0.361	8.08	0.632	15.11
Education	0.005	1.01	−0.031	−6.34
Married	0.091	2.30	0.054	1.35
Employment Status*				
self-employed	−0.083	−1.50	−0.110	−1.98
public employee	−0.041	−0.53	0.035	0.45
private employee	0.000	0.00	0.026	0.42
unemployed	−0.310	−3.81	−0.294	−3.63
retired	−0.082	−0.88	−0.030	−0.33
student	0.091	1.22	0.049	0.66
Pro-democracy dummy	−0.017	−0.48	−0.132	−3.63
Satisfaction with democracy	0.307	14.68	0.362	18.28
Pro-market attitudes	0.543	7.85	0.521	7.70
Inflation rate			−0.007	−4.96
Unemployment rate			−0.004	−0.75
Pseudo-R^2	0.058		0.027	
Number of obs.	14,255		11,197	

Notes: Ordered logit estimations with country dummies in (1) (country coefficients not shown) and without country dummies in (2).
* Omitted reference categories are not-married; and housewives or house/husbands.
Source: Authors' calculations from Latinobarometro.

Looking more closely at the *determinants* of attitudes about and satisfaction with democracy, we find that wealth and education levels have no significant correlation with satisfaction with democracy, but that they do have a positive and significant correlation with a preference for democracy over other systems, see Table 7.3. This is not surprising, in part because the same respondents that tend to be satisfied with their lives also tend to be satisfied with democracy, and in part because the educated may not

Table 7.3 Democracy: preferences and satisfaction

Latin America, 2000

Dependent Variable –>	Pro democracy dummy		Satisfaction with democracy dummy	
	Coeff.	*z-stat*	*Coeff.*	*z-stat*
age	0.018	2.606	−0.018	−2.881
age^2/100	−0.011	−1.374	0.025	3.561
male	0.135	3.409	−0.026	−0.748
log(wealth)	0.184	4.303	0.054	1.363
education	0.043	8.480	0.003	0.638
married	0.068	1.695	0.015	0.415
Employment Status*				
self-employed	−0.018	−0.335	−0.140	−2.827
public employee	0.120	1.493	0.124	1.758
private employee	0.103	1.633	−0.057	−1.021
unemployed	0.081	1.003	−0.133	−1.795
retired	0.094	1.030	−0.119	−1.484
student	0.356	4.612	−0.085	−1.236
Pseudo-R^2	0.063		0.065	
Number of obs.	14,879		14,357	

Notes: Respectively logit and ordered logit estimations with country dummies (coefficients not shown).
*Omitted reference category is housewives or house/husbands.

Source: Authors' calculations from Latinobarometro.

always be happier, but they are typically more discerning of the political system that they live with. Being self-employed has insignificant effects on preference for democracy, but it has negative and significant effects on satisfaction with democracy. One can imagine that a precariously employed individual in the informal sector might prefer democracy as a system, but not be particularly satisfied with how the government (or the economy) is performing.

The combined positive effects of pro-market attitudes and satisfaction with democracy on life satisfaction give us some cause for guarded optimism about a reinforcing virtuous circle in a region that has undertaken significant transitions in the economic and political realms: in the late 1980s and early 1990s, countries as different as Argentina and Guatemala, and Paraguay and Peru all undertook dual transitions to democracy and more market-oriented economies. These relationships seem to be fairly robust ones. Happier people are more likely than the average to support both systems. And while we cannot establish the direction of causality, my work on crisis with Sandip Sukhtankar (discussed in Chapter 6) suggests that individuals are able to distinguish between the systems per se and how they are working in particular countries and times. Economic crisis in particular seems to make those distinctions particularly clear.

Pettinato and I also looked at Russia. As in Latin America, having a pro-market attitude has positive and significant effects on happiness in Russia, suggesting that people in both regions who favor the ongoing turn to the market are in general more satisfied. Not surprisingly, having a pro-market attitude had significant and negative effects on the likelihood of respondents supporting redistribution, as did having positive prospects for the future (a high POUM). Age, meanwhile, had a positive and significant effect on restricting the incomes of the rich: support for redistribution seems to increase with age in Russia, likely reflecting the extent to which older people have both suffered more during the transition and are also more tied to a vision of the pre-transition social welfare system.[11]

Information about democratic attitudes in Russia was not comparable to that in the Latinobarometro. One question in the RLMS asks respondents whether they want to return to pre-Gorbachev (pre-*perestroika*) times.

---

[11] Regression results are reported in Graham and Pettinato (2002a).

Although a very crude indicator at best, this question was included in some of our regressions as a proxy indicator of respondents' preference for democracy over communism. We found that not wanting to return to communism, like having a pro-market attitude, had positive and significant effects on happiness. Again, the direction of causality is not clear, and it may well be that happy people are supportive of whatever policy environment they live in.

Still, there is some evidence of a virtuous pro-democracy, pro-market, happiness circle in Russia, as in Latin America. In Russia, however, that circle appears to be much smaller: 45% of respondents want to return to pre-*perestroika* days, while 75% of all respondents favor restricting the incomes of the rich. Ravallion and Loshkin find that redistribution in Russia is opposed not only by the rich, but also by the upwardly mobile poor.[12] Even so, because downward income mobility is so much more prevalent in Russia, 72% of all respondents in Russia support redistribution. In Latin America, only 44% of respondents favor redistribution over productivity, and 63% of all respondents think democracy is preferable to any other political system. The significant *upward*, as well as downward, mobility in Latin America may explain some of the differences in attitudes about markets, freedom, and redistribution between the region and Russia, where structural economic obstacles have been much harder to overcome, and the transition has been accompanied by increases in inequality that are likely unprecedented in modern times.[13]

---

[12] Ravallion and Lokshin (1999).

[13] The Gini coefficient in Russia increased from roughly 0.30 to 0.50, which is analogous to moving from Sweden to Brazil in inequality terms.

Adapting to Freedom and Friendships?

Helliwell and colleagues test for inter-regional differences on the effects of income, freedom, social connections—as measured by the importance of friendships and memberships in associations, among others—and corruption on well-being. They find that the income coefficient is weakest in Africa—most likely due to the likelihood of mis-measurement of the income variable and the importance of subsistence agriculture. The effects of social connections are lower in Asia and Africa and higher in Region 1 (the United States, Western Europe, Australia, and New Zealand) than in any other region. The negative effects of corruption are weakest in Asia and Africa and strongest in Region 1, as are the positive effects of personal freedom.

The well-being effects of corruption seem to be lower for those living in countries where corruption is a long-established feature of the status quo—and therefore people have become accustomed to it, while the well-being value attached to a sense of personal freedom is higher in societies classified as individualistic rather than collectivist. A recent paper by Ronald Inglehart and colleagues also finds that the well-being effects of freedom are greater in countries that have more of it and are more accustomed to it.[14]

Adapting to Bad Equilibrium: Crime and Corruption

In the same vein, Soumya Chattopadhyay and I examined the extent to which individuals adapt to and become more tolerant of high levels of crime and illicit activity (corruption). Our initial assumption is simply described by

---

[14] Inglehart et al. (2008).

the following vignette, based on my own experience. I grew up in Peru, but live in Washington, DC, for example. In Lima, I think nothing of removing my jewelry before going out on the street, nor of putting my briefcase on the floor rather than on the seat of the car so that my windows do not get smashed as I drive. In contrast, I would be outraged if I had to take similar precautionary measures when I step out of my Dupont Circle office (but would surely be more cautious in other parts of Washington, DC).

We used our pooled Latinobarometro data to test the extent to which the well-being effects of being a crime victim are lower—as are reporting rates—in countries in Latin America where crime rates are higher. As crime rates go up, citizens typically adapt, which is evidenced in lower reporting rates (reporting of petty crimes is less likely to result in corrective action as overall rates go up) and less stigma attached to being a victim. Nick Powdthavee's work on crime in South Africa suggests similar dynamics.[15]

If higher levels of crime and corruption are the norm, and individuals adapt to those norms and come to expect high levels of crime and corruption, as in Latin America, then it may be more difficult to generate the social and political support that is necessary for the difficult policy measures required to achieve a lower crime norm. We took advantage of the variance in levels of crime and corruption across Latin American countries as a means to test this proposition. We posit that understanding the important role of norms in individuals' responses to legal and institutional changes is likely an important part of the design of policies to reverse crime and corruption.

[15] Graham and Chattopadhyay (2009); Powdthavee (2005). For an overview of the interaction between behavior and institutions and the evolution of norms, see Bowles (2004); Young (1998).

Several papers in the burgeoning literature on happiness economics have documented the well-being costs associated with being a victim of crime or corruption. In this exercise, we build from the fairly standard assumption that these phenomena are negative for individual welfare, and query the extent to which the costs are mediated by norms of behavior, on the one hand, and adaptation, on the other. In other words, are the well-being costs of being a (petty) crime victim or of having to pay a bribe lower in contexts where these phenomena are more common?

The explanation for the variance in well-being costs could be twofold. On the one hand, if crime and corruption are the norm, then individuals would feel less stigmatized if they were the victim of petty crime, and less unethical if they had to engage in corruption to get things done. On the other, if crime and corruption are the norm, it is likely that individuals adapt to these phenomena, as well as to the associated costs, as common occurrences. So while individuals who live in countries where crime and corruption levels are high are likely to be less happy in general, there is less likelihood that they will be made unhappy specifically because of these phenomena.

We tested these assumptions econometrically, based on several years (1998–2008) of pooled Latinobarometro data—which provides us with information on happiness and on crime and corruption victimization (self-reported), on the one hand, as well as variance across and within countries and over time in the aggregate levels of these phenomena, on the other. Our approach entailed determining the likelihood that an individual would be a crime victim, based on the usual explanatory factors, such as his or her own socio-economic profile, plus the crime rate in the country that he or she lived in, plus whether or not he or she lived in a big city, and so on. We then isolated an 'unexplained' victimization probability, or the victimization that we were not able to explain with the above factors and used that probability as a proxy for differences in crime norms across respondents.[16]

Our intuition was that being a crime victim will have negative effects on happiness in any event, but that they will be lower when the unexplained victimization probability is higher. In other words, if you live somewhere where the crime norm is higher (like Lima versus Washington), then victimization will affect you less, both because of lower stigma and because you have already adapted to the increased likelihood that you will be a crime victim.

Our results support this intuition. First of all, our first-stage regressions yielded (expectedly) that those individuals who are older, more educated, wealthier, unemployed, speak the dominant language (e.g. non-minorities) and who live in a country with a higher crime rate, as well as those who were victimized in the past year, were more likely to be crime victims in the present year. In the second stage, we find that, as expected, controlling for everything else, being victimized in the past year has a

---

[16] Our basic econometric strategy was as follows. Our first-stage regression had the probability of being a crime victim (a logit equation, based on a yes–no crime victim question) as the dependent variable, and then a vector of controls for personal and socio-economic characteristics (including being unemployed or not and being a minority, yes or no), along with other factors that could explain crime victimization: the reported crime rate, lagged growth, the Gini coefficient, lagged crime victimization (individual crime victimization both one and two years ago), and controls for the size of the city respondents live in (small, medium, or large, with the idea that there is more crime in large cities), plus the usual error term. We isolated the resulting residuals (error terms) as each individual's unexplained crime probability—for example, the probability of being victimized that was not explained by objective traits. We then included that residual as an independent variable in a second-stage regression with happiness on the left-hand side, and the usual socio-demographic controls (including minority status) plus crime victimization on the right-hand side.

negative effect on happiness today. However, having a higher crime norm (or 'unexplained' victimization probability) is positively correlated with happiness—for example, it acts to counter or mitigate the negative effects of victimization, see Table 7.4.

In our study on optimism in Africa (reported in Chapter 3), Matthew Hoover and I examined the effects of adversity, such as crime victimization. We found similar evidence of downward adaptation. Optimism or positive attitudes presumably affect the way in which people deal with adversity. We examined the well-being costs of having been a crime victim. We split the sample into those respondents who reported high levels of personal security and those who reported low levels of personal security, with respondents' assessments of their living conditions as the dependent variable, and compared the coefficients on being a crime victim. We found that the costs were *lower* for those respondents who responded that they had *high* levels of insecurity than for those respondents who had *low* levels of insecurity, see Table 7.5.

There are several plausible explanations for this. On the one hand, if you expect that you will be a crime victim, some of those costs are already absorbed or adapted to in the expectations, and the actual event has less effect on well-being. Alternatively, victims of crime in an area where it is the norm are less likely to feel or suffer stigma effects than are those who are victims of crime in an area where crime is rare. Or perhaps the negative effects of being a crime victim are mediated by the higher levels of optimism that we find among the poor and more precariously situated. All three explanations could be at play.

Chattopadhyay and I repeated our econometric analysis of crime with identical regressions and the pooled Latinobarometro data, but with corruption victimization as the dependent variable. Like the crime question,

Table 7.4 Effects of crime and corruption on happiness in Latin America

Explanatory variables	Dependent Variable: happy							
age	−0.0230 (0.000)**	−0.0200 (0.000)**	−0.0210 (0.000)**	−0.0180 (0.005)**	−0.0230 (0.000)**	−0.0210 (0.000)**	−0.0230 (0.000)**	−0.0190 (0.003)**
age^2	0.0000 (0.000)**	0.0000 (0.000)**	0.0000 (0.000)**	0.0000 (0.000)**	0.0000 (0.000)**	0.0000 (0.000)**	0.0000 (0.000)**	0.0000 (0.035)*
gender	0.0070 −0.614	0.0210 (0.000)**	0.0400 (0.050)*	0.0240 −0.199	0.0100 −0.473	0.0410 (0.014)*	0.0500 (0.014)*	0.0470 −0.075
married	0.0850 (0.000)**	0.0600 (0.001)**	0.0630 (0.004)*	0.0620 −0.104	0.0840 (0.000)**	0.0620 (0.001)**	0.0710 (0.001)**	0.0690 (0.030)*
edu	−0.0220 (0.000)**	−0.0260 (0.000)**	−0.0280 (0.000)**	−0.0240 (0.000)**	−0.0240 (0.000)**	−0.0350 (0.000)**	−0.0400 (0.000)**	−0.0380 −0.129
edu^2	0.0010 −0.077	0.0010 (0.038)*	0.0010 (0.024)*	0.0010 −0.451	0.0010 −0.053	0.0010 (0.002)**	0.0010 (0.006)**	0.0020 −0.263
soccecon	0.2110 (0.000)**	0.2140 (0.000)**	0.2280 (0.000)**	0.2280 (0.000)**	0.2120 (0.000)**	0.2270 (0.000)**	0.2360 (0.000)**	0.2400 (0.000)**
subinc	0.2870 (0.000)**	0.3030 (0.000)**	0.3060 (0.000)**	0.3140 (0.000)**	0.2910 (0.000)**	0.3150 (0.000)**	0.3120 (0.000)**	0.3280 (0.000)**
ceconcur	0.2190 (0.000)**	0.1970 (0.000)**	0.2350 (0.000)**	0.2180 (0.000)**	0.2170 (0.000)**	0.1840 (0.000)**	0.2310 (0.000)**	0.2120 (0.000)**
unemp	−0.1770 (0.000)**	−0.2170 (0.000)**	−0.1990 (0.000)**	−0.2300 (0.002)**	−0.1680 (0.000)**	−0.2000 (0.000)**	−0.1890 (0.000)**	−0.2190 (0.001)**
poum	0.1750 (0.000)**	0.1410 (0.000)**	0.1470 (0.000)**	0.1530 (0.000)**	0.1760 (0.000)**	0.1580 (0.000)**	0.1690 (0.000)**	0.1730 (0.000)**
domlang	0.5950 (0.000)**	0.6520 (0.000)**	0.6360 (0.000)**	0.5490 (0.006)**	0.5970 (0.000)**	0.6680 (0.000)**	0.6450 (0.000)**	0.5880 (0.001)**

(cont.)

Table 7.4 (*Continued*)

Explanatory variables	Dependent Variable: happy				Dependent Variable: happy			
els			0.1000 (0.000)**				0.0970 (0.000)**	
vcrime	−0.0960 (0.000)**	−0.5360 (0.000)**	−1.0770 (0.000)**	−0.8930 −0.239				
crresid		0.4460 (0.000)**	1.0170 (0.000)**	0.8020 −0.286				
vcrime1 (1 year lag)			−1.4710 (10.77)**	−1.8190 −1.67				
vcrime2 (2 year lag)			1.8550 (15.52)**	1.6760 −1.47				
vcorr					−0.1570 (0.000)**	−0.9160 (0.000)**	−0.9070 (0.000)**	−1.1420 (0.017)*
corrresid						0.8090 (0.000)**	0.8330 (0.000)**	1.0340 (0.027)*
Control for gini	No	No	No	Yes	No	No	No	Yes
Control for GDP growth rate	No	No	No	Yes	No	No	No	Yes
Control for lagged GDP growth rates	No	No	No	Yes	No	No	No	Yes

Notes: Absolute value of z statistics in parentheses
* significant at 5%; ** significant at 1%.

Table 7.5 Costs of crime victimization in Africa

Regressions of living conditions on crime in Africa					
Only includes observations where personal security >= 3			Only includes observations where personal security < 3		
Observations	11675		Observations	3954	
LRchi^2(30)	1880.57		LRchi^2(30)	605.18	
Prob > chi^2	0.00		Prob > chi^2	0.00	
Pseudo R^2	0.05		Pseudo R^2	0.05	
L_Conditions	Coefficient	T-Score	L_Conditions	Coefficient	T-Score
Age	−0.0442***	−7.34	Age	−0.0370***	−3.71
Age^2	0.0003***	5.75	Age^2	0.0003***	3.08
Yeduc	0.0822***	8.06	Yeduc	0.0854***	4.79
Male	−0.0833***	−2.46	Male	−0.1164***	−2.00
Income	0.0794***	11.24	Income	0.0787***	6.41
Urban	−0.0098	−0.25	Urban	0.2278***	3.20
Unemployed	−0.0300	−0.75	Unemployed	−0.0363	−0.53
Freq_Crime_Victim	−0.0794***	−4.08	Freq_Crime_ Victim	−0.0459**	−2.43
Capeverde	0.3267***	4.58	Capeverde	0.0999	0.64
Namibia	0.8630***	11.02	Namibia	0.8255***	5.89
Nigeria	1.0310***	15.86	Nigeria	0.7854***	5.82
S. Africa	−0.0534	−0.76	S. Africa	−0.2786**	−2.45
Kenya	0.3875***	5.61	Kenya	0.5895***	5.46
Lesotho	−0.8754***	−10.77	Lesotho	−1.2125***	−9.92
Malawi	−1.1061***	−13.71	Malawi	−0.3532	−1.43
Mali	−0.1684***	−2.16	Mali	−0.2251	−1.21
Mozambique	0.8037***	10.22	Mozambique	0.3064**	2.39
Tanzania	−0.1136	−1.36	Tanzania	0.2647	2.14

Notes: Uganda is the dropped country dummy.
*Significant at the 10% level.
**Siginificant at the 5% level.
***Significant at the 1% level.
Source: Afrobarometer.

the first-order question is 'were you or someone in your family a victim of corruption in the past year', with possible answers, yes or no. There are also questions about concerns about corruption in the same data set, but these are more subjective and typically linked to other optimism variables.

We generated a similar corruption norm variable, based on the unobserved probability of being a corruption victim—as in the case of crime—and tested the extent to which it mediated the effects of corruption victimization on happiness.

We get virtually identical results. Being a victim of corruption in the past year is, not surprisingly, correlated with lower happiness levels. Our corruption norm variable, on the other hand, is positively correlated with happiness, see Table 7.4. As in the case of crime, being a victim of corruption is mitigated in contexts where corruption is more common, and there are both fewer stigma effects and individuals have adapted or become accustomed to it. Again, as in the case of crime, this adaptation is likely a good coping mechanism from an individual welfare perspective, but it also allows societies to remain in high corruption equilibriums for prolonged periods of time.

Conclusions

There are several ways to read these findings, as well as to judge whether adaptation is a good or bad thing for human welfare. Lower well-being costs are likely to make individuals more tolerant of or adaptable to such events, and thus less likely to do anything about it. At the same time, departing from a high crime/corruption norm is very hard—and potentially very costly—at the individual level. In other words, operating honestly in a situation where no one else does is inefficient and time-consuming in the best instance and dangerous or risky in the worst.[17] Thus, rather than operate 'irrationally' or

[17] Francisco Thoumi has written eloquently about the costs of diverting from corrupt practices, such as refusing to pay a bribe, where corruption is the norm. See Thoumi (1987).

in a costly manner, most individuals adapt to the higher crime norm. While that may be good for individual well-being—and perhaps survival—it may be negative in a collective sense, as it allows societies to fall into and stay in very bad equilibriums—such as the prolongation of very corrupt and/or violent regimes—for prolonged periods of time. These adaptation dynamics help explain why regimes, such as that of Mobutu in Zaire or Fujimori in Peru, were able to stay in power much longer than the predictions of most reasoned observers.

Our findings on the effects of both crime and corruption in Afghanistan—discussed in Chapter 3—support the adaptation hypothesis. Neither crime nor victimization due to corruption seems to have a significant effect on people's sense of well-being in Afghanistan, perhaps because people are used to both. But while this may be necessary in terms of coping strategies, it can surely not, as discussed above, be good for the overall welfare of the country.

Tipping such equilibrium is difficult at best, although it surely is possible, as evidenced by the highly visible case of Medellin, Colombia. Medellin had the highest murder rate—or at least one of the highest, accepting that these things are difficult to measure precisely—in the world in the early part of the millennium. After that, its crime rate tipped downward dramatically, due to a number of critical factors, including the leadership of a dynamic mayor, as well as crime rates reaching intolerable levels (the definition of tolerance obviously varies across populations). By 2008, citizens in Medellin had more confidence in their police than in any other city in the country, by a wide margin: 80% of respondents rather than 50% in other cities.[18]

---

[18] See Encuesta Annual Ciudadana Sobre Percepcion y Victimizacion.

In the same way that individuals adapt to the benefits (and also to the negative externalities) of overall rising income trends, they also adapt to the costs of rising crime and corruption trends. In the same way that income increases across time may not result in commensurate increases in well-being, increasing crime and corruption may not result in commensurate decreases in well-being as societies adapt to these phenomena.[19] There are surely tipping points in both instances, as levels of crime and corruption become unsustainable, for example, and/or as rising income levels result in positive externalities that increase happiness (and/or greed?).

In the end, understanding these dynamics is surely important to the crafting of legal and institutional solutions to reducing crime and corruption, and to strategies designed to change the behavior and attitudes of crime prevention authorities. It is an area where happiness or well-being surveys can add a great deal of information which is not captured by standard income or incidence-based measures.

---

[19] For a discussion of how people adapt and how these strategies may vary across socio-economic cohorts, see Di Tella et al. (2007).

CHAPTER 8

Happiness around the World

Lessons—and Questions—for Policy

All citizens are entitled to life, liberty, and the pursuit of happiness.

Constitution of the United States of America

In this book, I have explored the determinants of happiness across countries and cultures across the world. Understanding what makes people happy and why may help us understand some of the fundamental questions in economics. What is the relationship between happiness and income? Happiness and health? How do they differ in different countries and in different cultures at different stages of development? Would King Midas's greed for gold have had the same devastating effects if he had lived in a different time or place? On the basis of the research we have covered in this book, the answer is a resounding 'no'. In fact, what makes people happy seems to be remarkably similar in all sort of countries and contexts, from war-torn Afghanistan to new democracies like Chile and established ones like the United Kingdom.

Increasing levels of income—and income growth—tend to be accompanied by rising expectations and related frustrations (at the macro level, the paradox of unhappy growth, and at the micro level, our frustrated achievers), across a surprisingly wide range of countries at different economic development levels. At the same time, we also found that individuals across the globe were remarkably adept at adapting expectations downwards when necessary—our so-called happy peasants. In the same way that rising incomes (more gold) did not translate into ever increasing levels of happiness, remarkably adverse circumstances, such as high levels of crime and corruption or very poor standards of health, did not result in equivalently low levels of happiness. Happiness levels vary across countries and with economic and institutional conditions. Yet there is evidence of a great deal of upward and downward adaptation, as well as a clear role for innate character traits, in mediating the relationship between happiness and a range of environmental variables.

Surely deep deprivation makes people unhappy, while many things that accompany higher levels of development, such as better public goods and less disease, make people happier. Yet higher per capita income levels do not translate directly into higher average happiness levels. In part, this is because there are major differences in the nature of public goods and institutional regimes across countries. There are also cultural differences, which are difficult to measure. Part of the explanation lies in methodological issues: the relationship between income and happiness across countries depends a great deal on the type of happiness question that is used, and on the sample of countries and time frame that is selected for analysis. Environmental and institutional variables are also important to happiness, as are differences in the capacity of individuals to adapt to such contextual factors.

We have looked at several fundamental relationships across the world: happiness and income, happiness and economic development levels, happiness and health, happiness and macroeconomic regimes, and happiness and institutional regimes (good and bad). I also asked whether happiness mattered to future outcomes. My research—with several colleagues—suggests that happiness indeed has links to better outcomes in the labor market and health arenas, suggesting that causality could run in both directions: from income and better health to happiness, and from happiness to better labor market performance and to better health. This concluding chapter discusses the implications of what we have found for policy, as well as how and why some of what we find cannot be applied to policy at all.

Among other factors, our research highlights trends which are not typically identified by standard approaches—which assess welfare based on the information in consumption choices—but can have a major impact on human well-being or happiness. We paid particular attention to situations where individuals were unable to make choices to better their welfare and/or where choices were not optimal ones, but rather were driven by norms or by self-control problems. A major theme which runs through the book is the role of different norms and expectations in mediating the negative effects of some phenomena, such as ill health, crime and corruption, and the positive effects of others, such as freedom, friendships, and economic progress.

Adapting expectations downward in difficult contexts or at times of adversity, such as economic crises or rising rates of crime, seems to be a useful trait for preserving individual happiness in the face of major challenges. At the same time, it can result in lower collective welfare levels by increasing societal tolerance for bad equilibriums, such as high levels of crime and corruption or dysfunctional governments. Rising expectations in the context of economic progress or major improvements in health, in contrast, may actually reduce happiness, or at least require constantly increasing incomes or health improvements to keep well-being levels constant. At the same time, rising expectations may increase collective welfare by generating demand for better standards in areas such as health and education. Individuals' ability to adapt, meanwhile, is determined by some intersect between innate character traits (e.g. being naturally cheerful or curmudgeonly), on the one hand, and experience in the environment, on the other. At a minimum, these insights allow us to better understand how societies can be surprisingly tolerant—and happy—in the context of very bad conditions, and surprisingly critical—and unhappy—in the context of good conditions.

In the domain of individual income or economic status, one example of this kind of adaptation manifests itself in the happy peasant and frustrated achiever paradox: remarkably high levels of happiness among poor and destitute respondents coexisting with high levels of frustration among their counterparts who have experienced much more upward mobility. At the macroeconomic level, there is the related paradox of unhappy growth: controlling for individual wealth levels, respondents are unhappier in countries that have faster growth rates (the phenomenon is more important for countries that enjoy above average income levels and have above average growth rates). There are also institutional compon-ents. Institutions—ranging from political regimes to social networks—mediate the effects of economic progress on well-being. Yet their relative importance also varies depending on what norms and expectations are. Freedom, for example, seems to matter more to happiness in contexts where people are more accustomed to having it; phenomena, such as crime and corruption, in contrast, seem to matter less to happiness where they are more common.

Norms of health also vary: there seems to be very little relationship between individual satisfaction with health and objective indicators of health across countries (although within countries, the wealthy are typically more satisfied with their health than the very poor). The relationship between per capita incomes and health satisfaction seems analogous to the Easterlin curve, in which rising levels of per capita income do not translate directly into rising average happiness levels.

Health satisfaction and the effects of various health conditions on life satisfaction are also mediated by adaptation. Individuals are much better at adapting to physical conditions which are negative but stable than they are to those which are unpredictable, such as pain and anxiety, or epilepsy. And, as in the case of adaptation more generally, individuals' ability to adapt to such conditions is influenced by the intersection between the severity of the conditions and individual character traits. And it is hard to disentangle causality: more anxious people may suffer greater life satisfaction costs from being anxious, for example, while happier people are less likely to suffer from anxiety.

The obvious question, then, is how relevant is all of this for policy? What can policymakers take from these lessons? Can nations develop progress indicators based on the findings from happiness surveys? There is increasing discussion of using happiness surveys as a tool for public policy which complements income data, including happiness-based measures, such as national well-being accounts, as complements to national income accounts.[1] There are nascent efforts under way to consider and even to develop such

---

[1] In the United Kingdom, this effort has been led by scholars, such as Richard Layard and Paul Dolan, with a particular focus on the health arena. In France, there is an advisory group of academics including Joseph Stiglitz, François Bourguignon, Danny Kahneman, and Alan Krueger, among others.

217

measures in countries such as the United Kingdom and France.[2] Surely this is well ahead of traditional thinking. That alone is a positive development that can make us question how we are conceptualizing well-being and quality of life more generally.

But are we going too far? For all of their flaws, traditional welfare measures have been tested for years. While these measures can be criticized for oversimplifying the determinants of welfare or well-being, there is clarity in their simplicity. Income, simply put, is income and we do not need to spend a great deal of time analyzing the assumptions behind it, although there are extensive debates over how to measure it accurately. In the case of happiness, in addition to all of the difficulties associated with measuring it, there is extensive debate over its definition. How then can we use it as a policy tool?

Treading—Carefully—in the Policy Arena

Happiness research can make a number of potential contributions to policy. Yet a note of caution is necessary in directly applying the findings from this research, because of the potential biases in survey data, in particular the difficulties associated with analyzing it without being able to accurately account for unobservable personality traits. In addition, happiness surveys at times yield anomalous results which provide novel insights into human psychology—such as adaptation and coping during economic crises—but do not translate into viable policy recommendations.

One example is the finding (discussed above) that unemployed respondents are happier (or less unhappy) in contexts with higher unemployment

---

[2] Diener and Seligman (2004); Kahneman et al. (2004).

rates. The positive effect that reduced stigma has on the well-being of the unemployed seems to outweigh the negative effects of a lower probability of future employment.[3] One interpretation of these results for policy—raising unemployment rates—would obviously be a mistake. At the same time, the research suggests a new focus on the effects of stigma on the welfare of the unemployed.

Despite this note of caution, happiness surveys have great promise for helping us understand a variety of phenomena, many of them poverty-related, which cannot be explained by standard optimal choice or revealed preferences approaches. As noted in Chapter 1, two sets of questions come to the fore. The first of these is the welfare effects of macro and institutional arrangements that individuals are powerless to change, such as macroeconomic volatility, inequality, or weak governance structures. In contexts where access to political as well as economic opportunities are unequally shared, the poor in particular are least able to express their preferences (as they are the least able to either circumvent the system or vote with their feet and emigrate or put their assets abroad). Yet they may suffer negative welfare effects from inequality disproportionately.

The other set of questions are those in which behaviors are not the result of preferences, but of norms, addiction, or self-control problems. Any number of public health-related questions, such as obesity, cigarette smoking, and other phenomena, can and have been addressed by happiness surveys. Equally important are behaviors that are driven by low expectations. If the poor have low expectations for their own and their children's future—and if that is exacerbated by high and persistent levels of inequality as in Latin America—their decisions on any number of fronts, ranging from investing

---

[3] Clark and Oswald (1994); Eggers et al. (2006); Stutzer and Lalive (2004).

in their children's education to saving to public health attitudes—could be compromised. If those behaviors are merely analyzed as a result of revealed preferences or optimal choices, then the policy implications will be very different than if they are analyzed with greater awareness of the norms or constraints costs associated with the behaviors or choices.[4]

A second area of much promise for applying well-being surveys to policy is in the exploration and understanding of the importance of non-income variables, such as health, education, employment status, gender rights, environment, and any number of other variables to well-being and quality of life. Standard approaches, which rely on income-based measures of well-being, tend to underweight the importance of these variables. Happiness surveys tend to weight their importance differently, as well as allow us to assess their importance relative to each other.

Along those lines, the recent move to develop national well-being indicators in the United States, United Kingdom, and France is based on the assumption that happiness surveys can help us better gauge the relative weights of these variables, as well as track how those relative weights change over time across large samples. The intuition behind national well-being indicators is that well-being in these areas could be tracked and assessed in the same way and as a complement to the way GNP tracks income trends over time. It is an approach that holds much promise for providing broader measures of human welfare and well-being than income data alone can provide.

While there is certainly much potential for applying the results of happiness surveys to policy, three caveats in particular stand out. The first is a unifying theme in the book: the extent to which individuals adapt to many

[4] Graham (2008a); Graham and Ladkawalla (2006); Gruber and Mullainathan (2002).

situations, both upward and downwards. In the economic arena a number of studies suggest that people's expectations rise with rapid income growth and/or income gains and then drop with recessions and/or income losses. This will obviously affect trends in well-being indicators as economies change or cope with volatile international markets. Indeed, one of the most challenging issues is that while happiness levels do not seem to rise much with economic growth—and in fact may even fall with it in some contexts, as the paradox of unhappy growth suggests—happiness levels do fall significantly at times of crisis or other kinds of insecurity. As is noted above, it is difficult to say whether adaptation is a good or bad thing; that raises normative issues.

A related issue is the so-called happy peasant problem, which was alluded to above. In this instance, there are many cases where very poor and uninformed respondents, who happen to have a high set point (cheery nature), report they are very happy, even though they live in destitute poverty. The implications of this information for policy are very unclear. Should policy raise the peasant's awareness of how bad his or her situation is in order to raise expectations, although risking making them miserable? Should policy leave the peasant ignorant? How policy factors in set point/character differences is another difficult normative question. Should policy listen to the naturally unhappy respondents who have a tendency to complain more than to others? How much is expectations and how much is character, for example? Isn't policy too blunt an instrument to have influence on things that are primarily driven by character differences? How does one compare the peasant's high happiness levels with those of a millionaire—who not only has financial means that are above and beyond what the peasant could ever imagine, but also good health—but reports that he or she is miserable, due either to a low set point or to concerns about

221

relative differences with other millionaires. Certainly these differences go well beyond adaptation and are, instead, virtually incomparable. Yet both the peasant and the millionaire could be data points in the same happiness survey.

Another issue is cardinality versus ordinality. Happiness surveys are ordinal in nature and do not attach cardinal weights to the answers. Thus no distinction is made between the answers very happy and happy or happy and unhappy. Yet if these measures are really used to guide policy, does it become necessary to attach such weights? Does unhappiness matter more than happiness, for example? How does one choose between a policy that raises a happy person to very happy versus one that raises an unhappy person to just happy status? Many of these choices require normative judgments.

Perhaps a more fundamental question is whether happiness should be a policy objective. Are happy people successful or complacent, for example? There is some evidence that happier people, on average, perform better in the labor market and are healthier.[5] In other words, being happy seems to have positive causal effects on behavior. And very unhappy or depressed people have all sorts of related negative externalities. But the evidence also suggests that there is a top limit to this. Psychologists find that those that answer happiness questions near the top end of a ten-point scale are indeed more successful, but the effects are stronger around the seven to nine range rather than at the very top of the scale.[6] And there are certainly examples of very successful and creative people who are miserable for most of their lives. On average, though, it seems that happiness is correlated with better

---

[5] Graham et al. (2004).
[6] See Diener et al. (1999); Oishi et al. (forthcoming).

outcomes than is unhappiness or misery, and that eliminating the latter seems a worthwhile objective for policy.

The definition of happiness is fundamental to resolving these questions. At the same time, it is precisely the open-ended and undefined nature of the happiness question that makes it such a useful survey instrument and allows for comparisons across countries and cultures. The definition is not imposed on the respondent. Instead he or she is simply asked to assess his or her own happiness or life satisfaction in general terms. Thus, for survey purposes, the concept must remain undefined. In contrast, for policy purposes, some clarity on the definition seems necessary.

Attempting such a definition is clearly beyond the scope of this chapter—and of my expertise. Philosophers have provided a range of definitions over centuries. A more recent attempt to define happiness, by Charles and Anthony Kenny, seems particularly well suited to policy.[7] Kenny and Kenny define happiness as having three separate components: contentment, welfare, and dignity. Happiness defined simply as contentment seems an inappropriate objective for public policy. Yet, when it is defined as a combination of these three factors, it seems more relevant, particularly for many countries in which the major policy challenge is not extreme poverty but relative poverty, vulnerability, and inequality of income and opportunity.

Imposing a definition of happiness does not answer the question of how much weight policymakers should put on happiness as an objective versus others such as growth, policy reforms, and fiscal stability. There are inter-temporal considerations as well. Many reforms can and do make people unhappy in the short term, but in the long run are likely

---

[7] Kenny and Kenny (2006).

to guarantee them more prosperity and possibly greater happiness. There is a significant body of evidence, from both the behavioral economics and the happiness literatures, that individuals are loss averse and value losses disproportionately to gains. And the happiness literature shows that individuals adapt very quickly to income gains but much less quickly to losses, and more to changes in income than to changes in status.

There is also significant evidence of hyperbolic discounting—in other words, individuals trading off much larger future benefits for much smaller short-term ones. It is not a coincidence that most developed economies have forced savings schemes—whether individual accounts or pay-as-you go based—which are ultimately institutionalized mechanisms to get citizens to trade-off current consumption to save for their future retirement years. Our own work, meanwhile, suggests that high levels of inequality or low levels of social mobility, and related low expectations, can result in higher discount rates (and therefore more hyperbolic discounting) for those in the lower income ranks. This discounting can apply to areas such as public health as well as in the income realms, and may help explain why phenomena such as obesity are concentrated among lower income cohorts, at least in the developed economies.[8]

Certainly, understanding these behaviors is important information for policymakers. But can we use short-term happiness questions and measures as a gauge for policy? The information may be more useful for explaining lack of public support for optimal policies than it is as a guide to policy choice. Structural policy reforms, for example, can result in major changes in income and status, and related unhappiness for particular cohorts, at least in the short term, while producing gains in the aggregate in the long term.

[8] Felton and Graham (2005); Graham and Felton (2006a).

The example of Latin America provides a good illustration of the potential challenges.

As is discussed in Chapter 7, Latin America is a region that has for years suffered from the threat and the reality of populist politics and policies, which have primarily manifested themselves in fiscal profligacy for short-term political gain at the expense of longer-term investments in the structural changes in the macroeconomic and social policy realms that could generate sustainable growth and poverty reduction.[9] With the widespread turn to the market and acceptance of democratic institutions throughout most of the region in the 1990s, voting behavior seems to have matured and begun to resemble patterns in developed countries, in which voters are able to distinguish between the performance of particular governments and that of democratic and market systems per se. Despite significant shifts in the ideological spectrum and various leadership changes, there have been few real changes in economic policy in countries ranging from Chile and Brazil to Peru and El Salvador. There have also been cases of countries undergoing significant economic crisis and still retaining democratic institutions and some continuity in economic management, as in Argentina. In the majority of countries, patterns increasingly resemble retrospective voting, where voters judge past governments by their economic performance, and/or the patterns are influenced by some degree of party or ideological loyalty. Voters are, for the most part, also making the important distinction that characterizes mature democracy: that between support for systems of government and economic arrangements as opposed to support for specific governments in power.[10]

---

[9] See Dornbusch and Edwards (1991).
[10] Graham and Sukhtankar (2004); Lora and Olivera (2005); Stokes (1996); Weyland (2002).

At the same time, there are also significant pockets of political instability and increasing support for populist politicians and policies, such as in Bolivia, Ecuador, and Venezuela, where popular backlash against market reforms has also resulted in an erosion of democratic institutions. In these countries, the future of constitutional democracy as well as of pro-market policies is at risk. Inequality, meanwhile, remains a challenge that defies established policy prescriptions and likely undermines support for reform. Can surveys of happiness be of any use to policymakers in addressing such challenges in such a context?

Indeed, taken at face value, happiness surveys could, at least in theory, lend support to populist politicians. If the results of a national happiness survey show that the majority of citizens prefer inflation to unemployment, those results could fuel irresponsible fiscal policies in countries that are very vulnerable to hyperinflation (which indeed makes people very unhappy). The kinds of structural reforms that are necessary for long-term growth, meanwhile, are unlikely to be supported by a population that has a high tendency for hyperbolic discounting. How many voters will report that they are happier than before in the throws of a controversial privatization or tax reform, the benefits of which are not immediately clear, for example? How can happiness surveys be useful in such a context?

Surely there are risks to using the information that is in happiness surveys as a basis for policy. Yet our research also shows that economic crisis makes people very unhappy, and that happier people are more supportive of democracy and market reforms.[11] While the direction of causality is not clear (happier people may be more supportive of whatever policy context

---

[11] Graham and Sukhtankar (2004).

they live in), it does suggest that happiness is not inherently linked to support for irresponsible or anti-reform politics. And while we find that crisis reduces happiness, we also find that crisis is linked to decreased support for how markets and democracy are working, but to *increased* support for markets and democracies as systems.

This brief review underscores the difficulty of extracting a clear policy message from happiness surveys, particularly in volatile macroeconomic and political contexts. Yet there is a useful role for happiness surveys in such contexts, where there is often reform fatigue, risk and loss aversion due to past experience with macroeconomic volatility and other crises, and a large proportion of the population that is, at least in theory, vulnerable to hyperbolic discounting in helping us better understand and navigate the political outcomes that can result. Is it really irrational if one is poor and unemployed in an unstable developing economy, for example, to support an anti-system politician in the hope of change and a possible short-term improvement? Is it irrational for an individual in a fast-growing country, where rewards to different skill sets are changing rapidly and inequality is on the increase as a result, to feel insecure or unhappy? Understanding what makes people most unhappy with the policy context, via well-being surveys, might also help reformists avert the kind of policy mistakes that lead to populist or 'hyperbolic' politics.

Happiness and Policy Going Forward

As is discussed above, there are many reasons to be cautious about directly applying the results of happiness surveys to policy questions. Accepting those reasons, there is also a lot in happiness surveys—and in what we have

227

found in this exploration of happiness around the world—that *is* relevant to policy.

Many of the paradoxes that we find provide insights into the determinants of human well-being—whether they are directly applicable to policy or whether they simply highlight inconsistencies in what seems to make people happy. Understanding how and why humans adapt expectations upwards or downwards is ultimately an insight into human psychology. But it also helps us understand patterns of behavior, and why entire societies can remain in very bad social, economic, and political equilibrium—which may coexist with much better equilibrium in neighboring countries or states—for prolonged periods of time. Understanding these dynamics is surely a first step to going from bad to better equilibrium, in areas as varied as crime and corruption to poor health.

The happy peasant and frustrated achiever and unhappy growth paradoxes, meanwhile, highlight that the nature and pattern of growth matters a great deal, and that positive economic progress can be undermined very quickly by insecurity and inequality, among other things. Like all of the other institutional variables that we studied, these will vary across cultures and countries. While the effects of insecurity are more consistent and negative, the effects of inequality vary much more, depending on what inequality signals in particular contexts.

In addition to the conclusions from the research, happiness surveys can, in the end, tell us how the many aspects of human welfare compare to each other in relative terms. In the simplest sense, usage of these surveys can tell us how much each of these variables influences respondents' subjective and open-ended assessments of well-being. In a more complex conceptual sense, understanding the relative weights influence of different variables on reported well-being is part of the complex exercise of defining and measuring quality of life.[12]

This exercise—and its limitations—can also highlight areas where we need to know more to better understand human happiness and how we might use the findings from surveying it to develop better measures of quality of life. Ultimately these measures could complement standard income-based measures and, like income-based measures, be compared across countries and over time. Happiness surveys could help us track the effects of different policy arrangements, such as, for example, inflation versus unemployment and local versus central-level governments, on quality of life.

Happiness studies can provide critical insights into quality of life in areas including income, poverty and inequality, public health, and political arrangements. They can provide a method for gaining insights into many other questions, such as the effects of the environment or commuting time on quality of life. National well-being indicators, used cautiously, meanwhile, can be a good tool for tracking welfare, quality of life, and other well-being measures across countries and over time, and attaching relative weights to different variables. In the same way that GNP allows us to track economic growth within and across countries, national well-being measures provide a complementary tool for assessing welfare trends.

---

[12] From a technical standpoint, while it is not accepted practice to compare coefficients on equations based on categorical variables, as is the case with the ordered logits that are typically used for happiness studies, the results of OLS regressions on the same data and with the same specifications typically yield very similar results. The results of these can be used as a basis for attaching relative weights to the coefficients on independent variables, such as income and health.

At this stage, happiness economics has raised as many questions as it has answered. These include the implications of well-being findings for national indicators and economic growth patterns; the effects of happiness on behavior, such as work effort, consumption, and investment; and the effects on political behavior. In the case of the latter, surveys of unhappiness or frustration may be useful for gauging the potential for social unrest in various contexts. In order to answer many of these questions, researchers need more and better quality well-being data, particularly over time data for the same individuals, which allows for the correction of unobserved personality traits and correlated measurement errors, as well as for better determining the direction of causality (e.g. from contextual variables like income or health to happiness versus the other way around). These are major challenges in most happiness studies. Hopefully, the combination of better data and increased sophistication in econometric techniques will allow economists to better address these questions in the future, and increase the potential of such surveys to become a critical component of defining and measuring quality of life around the world.

From a personal standpoint, the study of happiness has opened the door to an intellectual journey that seems to have no bounds. I have found consistent patterns in the determinants of human well-being around the world, regardless of the economic and environmental context, and at the same time a remarkable human capacity to adapt to the most extreme of circumstances. That journey has demonstrated the limits that searching for gold has for happiness, and at the same time that income still matters to a number of things that mean a great deal to our happiness, such as good health. Equally important, the study of happiness provides a novel lens into human behavior and the intersect between psychology and economics, allowing for the exploration of all kinds of questions that are relevant to human well-being. The challenges for translating those insights into policy are daunting, but promise to be rewarding if in the end they enhance that well-being. I hope that the readers of this book have enjoyed this brief foray into that intellectual journey and possibly have the appetite for more.

REFERENCES

Adrianzen, B. and Graham, G. 1974. 'The High Costs of Being Poor.' *Archives of Environmental Health* 28: 312–15.

Alesina, A., Di Tella, R., and MacCulloch, R. 2004. 'Inequality and Happiness: Are Europeans and Americans Different?' *Journal of Public Economics* 88: 2009–42.

Aslund, A. 1995. *How Russia Became a Market Economy*. Washington: The Brookings Institution Press.

Bannerjee, A. and Duflo, E. 2007. 'The Economic Lives of the Poor.' *Journal of Economic Perspectives* 21(1): 141–62.

Benabou, R. and Ok, E. 1998. 'Social Mobility and the Demand for Redistribution: The POUM Hypothesis.' NBER Working Paper no. 6795, Cambridge, Mass.

Bertrand, M. and Mullainathan, S. 2001. 'Do People Mean What they Say? Implications for Subjective Survey Data.' *American Economic Review* 91: 67–72.

Birdsall, N. and Graham, C., eds. 2000. *New Markets, New Opportunities: Economic and Social Mobility in a Changing World*. Washington: The Brookings Institution Press and the Carnegie Endowment for International Peace.

Blanchflower, D. and Oswald, A. 2004. 'Well-Being over Time in Britain and the USA.' *Journal of Public Economics* 88: 1359–87.

Bowles, S. 2004. *Microeconomics: Behavior, Institutions, and Evolution*. Princeton: Princeton University Press.

Broome, J. 1999. *Ethics and Economics*. Cambridge: Cambridge University Press.

Cantril, H. 1965. *The Pattern of Human Concerns*. New Brunswick, NJ: Rutgers University Press.

Cardenas, M., Mejia, C., and Di Maro, V. Forthcoming. 'Education and Life Satisfaction: Perception or Reality?' in C. Graham and E. Lora, eds., *Paradox*

REFERENCES

and Perception: Measuring Quality of Life in Latin America. Washington: The Brookings Institution and the Inter-American Development Bank.

Case, A. and Deaton, A. 2005. 'Health and Wealth among the Poor: India and South Africa Compared.' *American Economic Review Papers and Proceedings* 95(2): 229–33.

Christakis, N. and Fowler, J. 2007. 'The Spread of Obesity in a Large Social Network over 32 Years.' *New England Journal of Medicine* 357(4), July 26.

Clark, A., Frijters, P., and Shields, M. 2008. 'Relative Income, Happiness, and Utility: An Explanation for the Easterlin Paradox and Other Puzzles.' *Journal of Economic Literature* 46(1), March: 95–144.

—— and Lelkes, O. 2009. 'Let Us Pray: Religious Interactions in Life Satisfaction.' Mimeo, Paris School of Economics, January.

—— and Oswald, A. 1994. 'Unhappiness and Unemployment.' *Economic Journal* 104: 648–59.

Cummins, R. A. and Nistico, H. 2002. 'Maintaining Life Satisfaction: The Role of Positive Cognitive Bias.' *Journal of Happiness Studies* 3: 45–62.

Deaton, A. 2004. 'Globalization and Health', in S. Collins and C. Graham, eds., *Brookings Trade Forum: Globalization, Poverty, and Inequality*. Washington: The Brookings Institution Press.

—— 2008. 'Income, Health, and Well-Being around the World: Evidence from the Gallup World Poll.' *Journal of Economic Perspectives* 22(2), spring: 53–72.

DeWan, P. and Christakis, N. 2009. 'Reference Group Effects on Individual Health: A Social Network Study of Relative Status.' Mimeo, Harvard Medical School, Health Care Policy Group, Cambridge, MA.

Diener, E. and Biswas-Diener, R. 2008. *Happiness: Unlocking the Mysteries of Psychological Wealth*. Boston: Blackwell-Wiley.

—— and Seligman, M. 2004. 'Beyond Money: Toward an Economy of Well-Being.' *Psychological Science in the Public Interest* 5(1): 1–31.

—— Sandvik, E., Seidlitz, L., and Diener, M. (1993). 'The Relationship between Income and Subjective Well-Being: Relative or Absolute?' *Social Indicators Research* 28: 195–223.

Diener, E., Suh, E. M., Lucas, R. E., and Smith, H. L. 1999. 'Subjective Well Being: Three Decades of Progress.' *Psychological Bulletin* 125: 276–302.

Di Tella, R., Galiani, S., and Shargrodsky, E. 2007. 'Crime Distribution and Victim Behavior during a Crime Wave.' Mimeo, Harvard University, Cambridge, MA., November.

REFERENCES

Di Tella, and MacCulloch, R. 2006. 'Happiness and Adaptation to Income and Status: Evidence from an Individual Panel.' Mimeo, Harvard University, Cambridge, MA.

—————— and Oswald, A. J. 2001. 'Preferences over Inflation and Unemployment: Evidence from Surveys of Happiness.' *American Economic Review* 91: 335–41.

Dolan, P. 1997. 'Modeling Valuations for Health States.' *Medical Care* 11: 1095–108.

—————— 2006. 'Happiness and Policy: A Review of the Literature.' DEFRA Report, Whitehall, United Kingdom.

Dornbusch, R. and Edwards, S., eds. 1991. *The Macroeconomics of Populism in Latin America*. Cambridge, MA.: MIT Press.

Duesenberry, J. 1949. *Income, Savings, and the Theory of Human Behavior*. Cambridge, MA: Harvard University Press.

Easterlin, R. 1974. 'Does Economic Growth Improve the Human Lot? Some Empirical Evidence', in P. David and M. Reder, eds., *Nations and Households in Economic Growth*. New York: Academic Press.

—————— 2001. 'Income and Happiness: Towards a Unified Theory.' *Economic Journal* 111: 465–84.

—————— 2003. 'Explaining Happiness.' *Proceedings of the National Academy of Sciences* 100(19): 11176–83.

—————— 2005. 'Feeding the Illusion of Growth and Happiness: A Reply to Hagerty and Veenhoven', *Social Indicators Research* 74(3): 429–43.

—————— 2008. 'Lost in Transition: Life Satisfaction on the Road to Capitalism.' *IZA Discussion Paper Series* 3049, March.

Eggers, A., Gaddy, C., and Graham, C. 2006. 'Well-Being and Unemployment in Russia in the 1990's: Can Society's Suffering be Individuals' Solace? *Journal of Socioeconomics* January: 209–42.

Epstein, J. and Axtell, R. 2006. *Growing Artifical Societies: Social Science from the Bottom Up*. Washington: The Brookings Institution Press/MIT Press.

Felton, A. and Graham, C. 2005. 'Variance in Obesity Incidence across Countries and Cohorts: A Norms Based Approach Using Happiness Surveys.' The Brookings Institution. Center on Social and Economic Dynamics Working Papers no. 45.

Frank, R. 1999. *Luxury Fever: Money and Happiness in an Era of Excess*. Princeton: Princeton University Press.

Frey, B. 2008. *Happiness: A Revolution in Economics*. Cambridge, MA: MIT Press.

REFERENCES

——and Stutzer, A. 2002a. *Happiness and Economics*. Princeton: Princeton University Press.

————2002b. 'What Can Economists Learn from Happiness Research?' *Journal of Economic Literature* 40: 401–35.

Friedman, B. 2005. *The Moral Consequences of Growth*. New York: Alfred Knopf.

Gaddy, C. and Graham, C. 2002. 'Why Argentina'02 is Not Russia '98.' *The Globalist* February. 12.

——and Ickes, B. 2002. *Russia's Virtual Economy*. Washington: The Brookings Institution Press.

Gardner, J. and Oswald, A. 2001. 'Does Money Buy Happiness? Some Evidence from Windfalls.' Mimeo. University of Warwick, Coventry.

Gerber, T. P. and Mendelson, S. E. 2002. 'How Russians Think about Chechnya.' PONARS Policy Memo no. 243. Washington: CSIS.

Gertler, P. and Gruber, J. 2002. 'Insuring Consumption against Illness.' *American Economic Review* 92(1): 50–70.

Graham, C. 2005. 'Some Insights on Development from the Economics of Happiness.' *World Bank Research Observer* September: 201–31.

——2007. 'Comments on Alejandro Gaviria: Social Mobility and Preferences for Redistribution in Latin America.' *Economia*, 8(1): 89–94.

——2008a. 'Happiness and Health: Lessons and Questions for Public Policy.' *Health Affairs* 27(1), January–February.

——2008b. 'Happiness Economics', in S. Durlauf and L. Blume, eds., *The New Palgrave Dictionary of Economics*, 2nd edn. Oxford: Palgrave Macmillan.

——and Chattopadhyay, S. 2008a. 'Gross National Happiness and the Economy.' *The Globalist* October 24.

————2008b. 'Public Opinion Trends in Latin America (and the US): How Strong is Support for Markets, Democracy, and Regional Integration?' Paper prepared for the Brookings Partnership for the Americas Commission, Washington, June.

————2009. 'How Much Can Citizens Adapt to Rising Crime? Some Evidence from Happiness Surveys from Latin America.' Mimeo, the Brookings Institution, Washington.

————and Picon, M. Forthcoming. 'The Easterlin and Other Paradoxes: Why Both Sides of the Debate May be Correct', in E. Diener, J. Helliwell, and D. Kahneman, *International Differences in Well Being*. Oxford: Oxford University Press.

235

REFERENCES

Graham, C., Eggers, A., and Sukhtankar, S. 2004. 'Does Happiness Pay? An Initial Exploration Based on Panel Data from Russia.' *Journal of Economic Behavior and Organization* 55: 319–42.

—— and Felton, A. 2006a. 'Does Inequality Matter to Individual Welfare: An Exploration Based on Happiness Surveys in Latin America.' *Journal of Economic Inequality* 4: 107–22.

—— —— 2006b. 'Complex Socio-economic and Political Changes in Central Asia: A Birds' Eye View from the Economics of Happiness.' Mimeo, Center on Social and Economic Dynamics, the Brookings Institution, Washington.

—— Hammond, R., and Young, P. 2007. 'Obesity and the Influence of Others.' *The Washington Post*, August 21.

—— Higuera, L., and Lora, E. 2009. 'Valuing Health Conditions across Cohorts, Countries, and Cultures: Insights from a New Method Based on Happiness Surveys.' Mimeo, the Brookings Institution, Washington (under review at *Health Affairs*).

—— and Hoover, M. 2007. 'Optimism and Poverty in Africa: Adaptation or a Means to Survival?' Afrobarometer Working Paper Series no. 76, November. Available at: <http://www.afrobarometer.org>.

—— and Ladkawalla, D. 2006. 'Cheap Food, Societal Norms, and the Economics of Obesity.' *The Wall Street Journal*, August 25.

—— and Lora, E. Forthcoming. 'Health Perceptions and Quality of Life in Latin America', in C. Graham and E. Lora, eds., *Paradox and Perception: Measuring Quality of Life in Latin America*. Washington: The Brookings Institution and the Inter-American Development Bank.

—— and Pettinato, S. 2002a. *Happiness and Hardship: Opportunity and Insecurity in New Market Economies*. Washington: The Brookings Institution Press.

—— —— 2002b. 'Frustrated Achievers: Winners, Losers, and Subjective Well-Being in New Market Economies.' *Journal of Development Studies* 38(4): 100–40.

—— and Sukhtankar, S. 2004. 'Does Economic Crisis Reduce Support for Markets and Democracy in Latin America? Some Evidence from Surveys of Public Opinion and Well-Being.' *Journal of Latin American Studies* 36: 349–77.

—— and Young, P. 2003. 'Ignorance Fills the Income Gulf.' *The Boston Globe*, June 23.

Granovetter, M. 1973. 'The Strength of Weak Ties.' *American Journal of Sociology* 78, May: 1360–79.

REFERENCES

Grootaert, C. and van Bastelaer, T., eds. 2002. *The Role of Social Capital in Development: An Empirical Assessment*. Cambridge: Cambridge University Press.

Gruber, J. and Mullainathan, S. 2002. 'Do Cigarette Taxes Make Smokers Happier?' NBER Working Paper no. 8872, Cambridge, MA.

Hammond, R. and Epstein, J. 2007. 'Exploring Price Independent Mechanisms in the Obesity Epidemic.' CSED Working Paper no. 48, the Brookings Institution, July.

Hausman, D. 2007. 'What's Wrong with Health Inequalities?' *The Journal of Political Philosophy* 15(1).

Helliwell, J. 2003. 'Well-Being and Social Capital: Does Suicide Pose a Puzzle?' Unpublished manuscript. Vancouver: University of British Columbia.

—— 2008. 'Life Satisfaction and Quality of Development.' Mimeo, University of British Columbia.

—— Haifang Huang, H., and Harris, A. 2008. 'International Differences in the Determinants of Life Satisfaction.' Mimeo, University of British Columbia.

Herrera, J. and Roubaud, F. 2005. 'Dynamique de la pauvreté urbaine au Pérou et à Madagascar 1997–1999: Une Analyse sur données de panel.' Ibero America Institute for Economic Research (IAI) Discussion Papers 106. Ibero-America Institute for Economic Research.

Howell, R. T. and Howell, C. J. 2008. 'The Relation of Economic Status to Subjective Well-Being in Developing Countries: A Meta-Analysis.' *Psychological Bulletin* 134(4): 24–67.

Hudson, J. 2006. 'Institutional Trust and Subjective Well-Being across the EU.' *Kyklos* 59: 43–62.

Inglehart, R. 1988. 'The Renaissance of Political Culture.' *American Political Science Review* 82, December: 1203–30.

—— Foa, R., Peterson, C., and Welzel, C. 2008. 'Development, Freedom, and Rising Happiness: A Global Perspective (1981–2007).' *Perspectives on Psychological Science* 3(4): 264–85.

Inter-American Development Bank. 2008. *Beyond Facts: Understanding Quality of Life in Latin America*. Washington: Inter-American Development Bank.

Kahneman, D., Diener, E., and Schwarz, N. 1999. *Well-Being: The Foundations of Hedonic Psychology*. New York: Russell Sage.

—— Krueger, A., Schkade, D., Schwarz, N., and Stone, A. 2004. 'Toward National Well-Being Accounts.' *AEA Papers and Proceedings* 94: 429–34.

REFERENCES

Kenny, A. and Kenny, C. 2006. *Life, Liberty and the Pursuit of Utility: Happiness in Philosophical and Economic Thought*. London: Imprint Academic.

Kingdon, G. and Knight, J. 2007. 'Communities, Comparisons, and Subjective Well Being in a Divided Society.' *Journal of Economic Behavior and Organization* 64(1), September.

Klugman, J. and Braithwaite, J. 1998. 'Poverty in Russia during the Transition: An Overview.' *World Bank Research Observer* 13: 37–58.

Knight, J. and Gunatilaka, R. 2007. 'Great Expectations? The Subjective Well Being of Rural-Urban Migrants in China.' Discussion Paper Series no. 322, Department of Economics, University of Oxford, April.

Labonne, J. and Chase, R. 2008. 'So You Want to Quit Smoking: Have You Tried a Mobile Phone?' Policy Research Working Paper Series no. 4657, the World Bank, June.

Layard, R. 2005. *Happiness: Lessons from a New Science*. New York: Penguin Press.

Lora, E. and Chaparro, C. Forthcoming. 'The Complex Relation between Satisfaction and Income', in C. Graham and E. Lora, eds., *Paradox and Perception: Measuring Quality of Life in Latin America*. Washington: The Brookings Institution and the Inter-American Development Bank.

—— and Olivera, M. 2005. 'The Electoral Consequences of the Washington Consensus.' *Economia* 5(2), spring: 241–66.

Lowenstein, G., Prelec, D., and Weber, R. 1999. 'What, Me Worry? A Psychological Perspective on the Economics of Retirement', in H. Aaron, ed., *Behavioral Dimensions of Retirement Economics*. Washington: The Brookings Institution Press, 215–52.

Luengas, P. and Ruprah, I. 2008. 'Should Central Banks Use Happiness Surveys for Inflation Targeting?' Mimeo, Inter-American Development Bank.

Luttmer, E. 2005. 'Neighbors as Negatives: Relative Earnings and Well Being.' *Quarterly Journal of Economics* 120(3), August: 963–1002.

Marmot, M. 2004. *The Status Syndrome: How Social Standing Affects our Health and Longevity*. London: Bloomsbury Press.

Oishi, S., Diener, E., and Lucas, R. E. Forthcoming. 'The Optimum Level of Well-Being: Can People be Too Happy?' *Perspectives on Psychological Science*.

Oswald, A. 1997. 'Happiness and Economic Performance.' *Economic Journal* 107: 1815–31.

—— and Powdthavee, N. 2007. 'Obesity, Unhappiness, and the Challenge of Affluence: Theory and Evidence.' *Economic Journal*, 117(521): 441–54.

REFERENCES

Picon, M. 2008. 'Explaining Subjective Well Being by Objective Well Being Measures: An Application for Latin America.' Mimeo, the Brookings Institution, Washington.

Pigou, A. G. 1920. *The Economics of Welfare*. London: Macmillan.

Powdthavee, N. 2005. 'Unhappiness and Crime: Evidence from South Africa.' *Economica* 72: 531–47.

Powdthavee, N. Forthcoming. 'Happiness and Standard of Living.' *Economica*.

Preston, S. 1975. 'The Changing Relation between Mortality and Level of Development.' *Population Studies* 29(2): 239–48.

Puri, M. and Robinson, D. 2005. 'Optimism and Economic Choice.' NBER Working Paper no. 11361, May.

Ravallion, M. and Lokshin, M. 1999. 'Who Wants to Redistribute? Russia's Tunnel Effect in the 1990s.' Policy Research Working Paper no. 2150. Washington: World Bank, July.

———— 2005. 'Who Cares about Relative Deprivation Effects.' Policy Research Working Paper Series no. 3782, the World Bank, Washington, December. Available at: <http//:ideas.repec.org/p/wbk/wbrwps/3782.html>.

Rios, J. and Godoy, J. 2007. 'Personal Freedom, Self-Concept, and Well-Being among Residents of Havana and Santiago, Cuba.' Paper presented to the First Latin American Congress of Public Opinion, Colonia del Sacramento, Uruguay, April. 12–14.

Rojas, M. 2004. 'Well-Being and the Complexity of Poverty.' Research Paper no. 2004(2). Helsinki: World Institute for Development Research.

Sen, A. 1995. 'Rationality and Social Choice.' *American Economic Review* 85: 1–24.

Shaw, J., Johnson, J., and Coons, S. 2005. 'U.S. Valuation of the EQ-5D Health States: Development and Testing of the D1 Valuation Model.' *Medical Care* 43(3), March: 203–20.

Soroka, S. N., Helliwell, J., and Johnson, R. 2007. 'Measuring and Modelling Interpersonal Trust', in F. Kay and R. Johnson, eds., *Diversity, Social Capital, and the Welfare State*. Vancouver: UBC Press.

Stevenson, B. and Wolfers, J. 2008. 'Economic Growth and Subjective Well-Being: Re-assessing the Easterlin Paradox.' *Brookings Panel on Economic Activity*, April.

Stiglitz, J. 2002. *Globalization and its Discontents*. New York: W.W. Norton and Co.

Stokes, S. 1996. 'Public Opinion and Market Reforms: The Limits of Economic Voting.' *Comparative Political Studies* 29(5): 499–519.

REFERENCES

Stutzer, A. and Lalive, R. 2004. 'The Role of Social Work Norms in Job Searching and Subjective Well-Being.' *Journal of the European Economic Association* 2: 696–719.

Thoumi, F. 1987. 'Some Implications of the Growth of the Underground Economy.' *Journal of Inter-American Studies and World Affairs*, 29(2): 189–216.

Van Praag, B. and Ferrer-i-Carbonell, A. 2004. *Happiness Quantified: A Satisfaction Calculus Approach*. Oxford: Oxford University Press.

Veenhovern, R. 2000. 'Freedom and Happiness: A Comparative Study of 46 Nations in the Early 1990s', in E. Diener and E. Suh, eds., *Culture and Subjective Well Being*. Cambridge, Mass.: MIT Press.

Weyland, K. 2002. *The Politics of Market Reform in Fragile Democracies: Argentina, Brazil, Peru, and Venezuela*. Priceton: Princeton University Press.

Whyte, M. and Hun, C. 2006. 'Subjective Well Being and Mobility Attitudes in China.' Mimeo, Harvard University, Cambridge, MA.

Young, P. 1998. *Individual Strategy and Social Structure: An Evolutionary Theory of Institutions*. Princeton: Princeton University Press.

SURVEYS

Afrobarometer Survey (Africa). Available at <http:www.afrobarometer.org>.

Encuesta Annual Ciudadana Sobre Percepcion y Victimizacion en las Seis Ciudades Mas Grandes del Pais. Fundacion Seguridad y Democracia, Bogota, Colombia. Available at: <http://www.seguridadydemocracia.org>.

Gallup World Poll. Available at: <http://www.gallup.org>.

General Social Survey (GSS) for the USA. Available at: <http://www.norc.org/projects/General+Social+Survey.htm>.

Latinobarometro Survey (Latin America). Available at: <http://www.latinobarometro.org>.

Russian Longitudinal Monitoring Survey (RLMS). Available at: <http://www.cpc.unc.edu/projects/rlms/>.

Veenhoven, R. 2002. World database of happiness [online]. Available at: <http://www2.eur.nl/fsw/research/happiness/index.htm>, accessed 17 June 2005.

INDEX

INDEX

INDEX

INDEX